Doing Business with
Qatar

MISC.

PAID

INFORMATION

S TO PAY

To open doors,
you need open minds.

Talk to Ahli United Bank.

When you want to do business in Bahrain you need an authoritative partner that has first hand knowledge of business trends and practices in the region. Ahli United Bank is one such bank.

Innovative by nature, AUB offers clients strategic solutions, backed by a dynamic structure that offers clients access to regional and global opportunities. Formed to create a financial bridge between the Middle East and global markets the bank has extensive product skills, sophisticated technology and the highest standards of customer service.

Take the first step to doing successful business in Bahrain. Call Ahli United Bank.

Ahli United Bank
PO Box 2424, Manama, Bahrain.
Telephone (+973) 220 555
Facsimile: (+973) 220 552
info@ahliunited.com

Doing Business with
Qatar

Consultant Editor:
Philip Dew

Middle East Series Editor:
Anthony Shoult

With contributions from
Jonathan Wallace

Foreword by:
David Wright
HM Ambassador

in association with

TRADE
PARTNERS UK
www.tradepartners.gov.uk

ahli united bank

KOGAN
PAGE

Publisher's note

Every possible effort has been made to ensure that the information contained in this handbook is accurate at the time of going to press, and the publishers and authors cannot accept responsibility for any errors or omissions, however caused. No responsibility for loss or damage occasioned to any person acting, or refraining from action, as a result of the material in this publication can be accepted by the editor, the publisher or any of the authors.

British Library Cataloguing in Publication Data

ISBN 0 7494 3813 4

Typeset by JS Typesetting Ltd, Wellingborough, Northants
Printed and bound in Great Britain by Biddles Ltd, *www.biddles.co.uk*

Contents

Part Three: Company Operational Issues

Part Four: The Fiscal and Regulatory Framework

Part Five: The Financial Structure and Banking System

Part Eleven: Appendices

Foreword

The merchants of Qatar have given British exporters a warm welcome for the last 30 years. Britain has been among its leading suppliers ever since Qatar became a State in 1971. The network of business relationships that has built up over the years provides British exporters with an enormous advantage over their competitors, particularly in a market where contacts and relationships are the fundamental building blocks of any business opportunity.

Qatar is currently enjoying a spurt in economic growth as a result of the government's success in investing in the development of its massive gas reserves. Its gas income will soon equal income from oil. Liquefied natural gas apart, Qatar now has a growing range of downstream chemical industries, which is adding more value to its gas income. A programme of privatization of government assets is also improving bureaucratic efficiency. These immensely strong economic fundamentals offer British exporters every opportunity for profitable business.

Every market has its peculiarities. I hope that *Doing Business with Qatar* will help you to fill in these gaps. It should be particularly useful for businessmen and women who are new to the area and I hope it will encourage you to include Qatar in your Gulf itinerary.

David Wright
HM Ambassador
19 January 2002

AHLI UNITED BANK (AUB)

Ahli United Bank – the creation of a substantial international financial group from two successful banking institutions.

Ahli United Bank (AUB) does not merely constitute a larger version of United Bank of Kuwait (UBK) or Al-Ahli Commercial Bank (ACB), but a stronger and better institution altogether, with fresh challenges and greater growth potential than both predecessors. AUB now offers a more diversified product range, reaches a wider client base and has a broader geographical presence.

AUB is a fully-fledged commercial institution and investment bank providing wealth management, retail, corporate treasury, offshore and private banking services. It is geared towards growth through the development of a larger client base in the GCC states and of close partnership with customers, staff and product providers.

By continuing to focus on our clients' needs and relying on management's professional skills, we aim to achieve excellent performance for our shareholders on a year-by-year basis.

In addition to our stated intention of growing through mergers and acquisitions, the Bank's size and ability to move swiftly make it perfectly suited to a strategy of systematic growth, improved liquidity, greater market capitalization and enhanced quality of earnings.

It is intended to achieve this through fully utilizing AUB's larger geographical footprint and distribution network, and providing a high quality service to our customers through a wider portfolio of commercial and investment banking services. At the same time, streamlining our business will instill even greater financial discipline as we enter new markets, enhancing out technological capabilities and continuing to apply a very effective risk management strategy.

AUB is a commercially-driven organisation, committed to providing the highest levels of service to an increasing customer base, and to planned evolution through both organic growth and acquisitions. The Bank has brought together an experienced and talented professional team, dedicated to implementing management's vision through the application of market expertise and the latest technology.

Headquartered in Bahrain, the AUB Group operates within the regulatory framework of the Bahrain Monetary Agency (BMA), whilst its UK subsidiary is regulated by the Financial Services Authority (FSA) and investment Management Regulatory Organisation (IMRO).

The Bank employs some 500 staff in Bahrain, London, Kuwait, Dubai and the Channel Islands.

AUB's revenue business is organized into two divisions: Private Banking and Wealth Management and Commercial Banking and Treasury. The Risk, Finance and Strategic Development Group supports both these divisions and is responsible for the Group's expansion through mergers and acquisitions. The Regulatory and Support Group is responsible for internal and external compliance, and corporate governance issues.

Private banking is a key strategic element in AUB's expansion plans. This division includes all the non capital-intensive sectors of the business, offering customers an integrated wealth management service based on performance and a balanced product mix. Private banking combines discreet, personal care with expert financial support, ensuring that each client enjoys services catering to their individual scenario.

AUB private banking offers a comprehensive product portfolio including standard banking, investments and finance services, tax, inheritance and trust advice, along with wealth protection, structured lending and foreign exchange services. We also offer a wide range of traditional funds and alternative investment vehicles. Continuing improvements in methodology and concerted efforts in each Gulf market keep AUB's products at the forefront of investment solutions.AUB provides an innovative range of Asset Management products that reflect the Bank's customer focus. When looking to introduce investment management services to its Middle East operations, AUB established a joint venture with Mellon Global Investments. The new entity, Mellon Ahli Asset Management Ltd offers a wide range of services, including equity and debt management, complemented by total return hedge funds and capital protected structures. Crucially, the new structure allows AUB to focus its attention on client relationships whilst continually enhancing the available product portfolio.

Continued product innovation and greater access to customers in the Gulf has sustained steady progress in Islamic Banking area. AUB's range of Sharia'a based services provides a complementary option to the Bank's conventional product portfolio. Consistency in both quality and breadth of service means that GCC customers now have access to standard and sophisticated international banking and fund management services through their existing network. AUB also offers Morabaha services to corporations, providing money market type facilities in a Sharia'a compatible structure involving short-term trade financing with deferred settlement.

By recently initiating a new joint venture with Henderson Global Investors, a specialist in international real estate fund management, AUB is able to introduce more of its clients to the lucrative European markets. The result is a higher level of product quality which, supported by AUB's global resources and substantial technical expertise, makes for one of the most innovative property investment services available.

The Bank's traditional role as a key financial link was further supplemented by improved access to more Middle East markets for European exporters and we now enjoy a significant further commercial advantage in the ability to offer a service that is individually tailored as well as highly competitive.

For many years UBK has acted as a key financial link for European exporters seeking access to Middle Eastern markets, while AUB Bahrain has worked with clients in the Gulf region, including major private companies, financial institutions and the government. These two perspectives mean AUB can now identify greater opportunities in more markets – a trend that evolves as the Bank continues to build new corporate relationship in manufacturing, construction, trade and tourism throughout the region.

Structured Finance activities encompass three business lines. Acquisition finance – a dedicated team focuses on the origination of transactions derived from corporate merger and acquisitions activity. Collateralised obligations – in the high growth securitisation market the Bank can play significant role in the credit enhancement of special purpose structures. Bespoke project financing – primarily an advisory and structuring service for project sponsors.

The group's Treasury operations in Bahrain and London incorporates all the components essential to successful treasury management – innovative services, leading-edge technology, quality execution and resources. AUB's treasury management unit in Bahrain coordinates the group's proprietary trading and the provision on a wide range of products and services for a customer base including regional and local banks, corporates, institutions and high-net-worth investors.

These services include the quoting and trading of all major currencies including Gulf and regional currencies, deposits in all major currencies for all maturity periods, structured deposit accounts and a round-the clock foreign exchange service. We manage global interest rate risk on behalf of corporates and quote forward rate agreements, interest rate swaps, interest rate caps, collars and floors. In London treasury specializes in money market services and off-balance sheet instruments.

The Aviation Finance provides specialist finance to airlines and aircraft leasing companies around the world. Over the years the bank has earned a reputation for market knowledge, acumen and experience, and a significant client base has been developed in what is a highly specialized field. The Bank provides finance secured on commercial aircraft to operating lessors, either as a sole lender or as part of a syndicate. Our knowledge of this sector enabled the Bank to avoid any diminution in value in its investments after the September 11th events.

The Bank offers a competitive range of mortgage products, which it reviews continually, for property ventures in the office, retail and industrial sectors. The Bank is an experienced participant in international property finance and investment and has recently pioneered a series of commercial property securitisations in the UK. Joint venture financing proposals are considered, and the standard range of services includes investment loans secured on single assets or portfolios, mezzanine loans on the same basis and pre-let and speculative development finance.

The Bank provides a competitive and innovative range of mortgage products which it reviews continually to ensure consistent quality in an ever-changing marketplace. The Bank adheres to the highest lending standards and is a member of the Council of Mortgage Lenders. The Bank provides a fast and efficient service to individuals resident in the UK or overseas, trusts and corporate bodies.

Both UBK in London and AUB Bahrain offer a range of personal banking services which, over time, have anticipated and satisfied the needs of customers in each location. However, being committed to providing quality services means offering more than core products such as savings, current, deposit and fixed deposit accounts, or loans, credit cards and off-shore facilities. UBK offers first-class banking and investment services for Gulf nationals with business or personal interest in the UK and continental Europe. All activities are designed to support and complement the Bank's wealth management and investment services. With a network consisting of thirteen branches across the country, AUB Bahrain provides the full range of personal banking services.

In the first half of 2001, AUB announced two acquisitions which were powerful expressions of the Bank's strategy and significantly advance its regional aspirations.

In March 2001, AUB acquired a significant minority share in Bank of Kuwait and the Middle East (BKME) currently 18%.

In June 2001, AUB announced the merger of its wholly-owned subsidiary, Al-Ahli Commercial Bank, with Commercial Bank of Bahrain (CBB), formerly Grindlays Bahrain Bank Bsc. The combined entity has an approximate 21% share of the Bahrain onshore banking market and became fully operational on October 2001.

AUB has also established a joint venture with Mellon Global Investments, Mellon Ahli Asset Management Limited (Mellon Ahli), to offer investment management services in the Middle East, and a strategic alliance with United Bank of Kuwait and Henderson Global Investors to become the leading provider of real estate investment products in the Middle East.

These recent developments reflect AUB's determination to create a dynamic structure that offers its regional clients leading-edge financial opportunities, allied with the highest standards of customer service.

As a new bank in the Arab world with established roots, AUB is defining a fresh identity in the marketplace, creating organic growth and using mergers and acquisitions to bring consolidation to an oversaturated financial services sector.

A key component in fulfilling this strategy is the quality of our management team and the discipline with which we run our business. Our strengths are vision, focus and commitment.

The Group will realize significant operating efficiencies by leveraging technology platforms as we grow both domestically and internationally. These platforms will make it possible to expand sales of our products and enter new markets at a lower cost. At all times, we will remain customer focused and, looking forward, we will provide clients with an even greater range of solutions, becoming a more strategic part of their lives and decision making process.

At the core of the Bank's strategic planning are two key concepts. Firstly: complementarity – of customers, products, service, expertise and resources; and secondly: synergy – of people, markets and objectives. The Bank's faith in these attributes has proved to be well founded, and the future looks extremely promising as the potential of the demographically attractive Gulf customer base is matched by an enhanced product repertoire and distribution network. This will be further reinforced through the mobilization of AUB's marketing expertise to capitalize on acknowledged reputation for product, technological and corporate initiatives in identified business sectors based on the long standing involvement of its subsidiary bank in the region.

List of Contributors

Abu-Ghazaleh Intellectual Property (AGIP) has been a pioneering force in the implementation of intellectual property protection in Arab countries. Since 1972, the firm has been serving the needs of the world's leading companies as they seek protection for their trademarks in the region, while also lending expertise to Arab governments as they attempt to develop intellectual property laws. **AGIP** provides trademark, patent and copyright registrations along with experienced legal representation before high courts for any opposition, cancellation and appeal actions.

Headquartered in Amman, Jordan, **AGIP** supports branch offices in 33 Arab countries and the Chairman's office in Cairo, Egypt. The company operates worldwide through special correspondents.

Sami Shafi Younis is Manager-in-Charge of Abu-Ghazaleh Intellectual Property in Doha. He has a degree in English from Qatar University and is a member of INTA, the International Trademark Association.

Dr Ghanim AlHammadi has been General Manager of **Doha Securities Market** (DSM) since September 2001, prior to which he held a number of posts in government. He is a member of the board of directors of Qatar National Bank and of the College of Administration and Economics at the University of Qatar. His PhD was obtained in Engineering Management from George Washington University in Washington DC, where he had previously studied for an MSc in Information Management and BSc in Electrical Engineering, Computer Engineering Option.

Apollo Enterprises commenced operations in 1980 with real estate and furniture divisions. Since that time, the company has expanded into other areas including blasting and painting, scaffolding and chemicals. Today **Apollo**, one of the longest-established real estate agencies in Doha, is the undoubted market leader in the provision of both short- and long-term accommodation for expatriates.

Simon King is manager of Apollo Enterprises Real Estate Division. He has been resident in Doha for over 10 years and has more than five years' experience of working in the country's property sector.

ASA Consulting is a UK-based independent marketing-focused consultancy specializing in the Middle East region. The firm provides a wide range of consultancy services across industrial sectors, either directly or through affiliated organizations, to both international and local public and private sector agencies and organizations. The services provided include assistance to investors in specific areas such as market research and investigations for technical and industrial products and services and techno-economic feasibility studies to the highest standards.

David Chaddock is a Chartered Electrical Engineer specializing in commercial management. He has spent more than 30 years primarily working for multinational manufacturing companies in developing markets. He has spent the last five years in Qatar working as a Management Consultant.

The **Commercial Bank of Qatar (CBQ)** was established in 1975, with an initial capital value of QR10 million, as the first wholly-owned private commercial bank in Qatar. In little more than 25 years, it has grown to become a leading regional bank, with capital and reserves in excess of QR660 million, and assets totalling QR5.2 billion in value.

With the growth in export revenues, and resulting opportunities in project and syndicated banking locally and internationally, Corporate Banking has developed into a core business for CBQ with the bank being a regular participant in all local syndicated lending. Qatar's economic strength and ambition to position itself as a major commercial power in the Middle East will greatly impact this sector of its business in the years ahead, and the Bank has geared up to capitalize on these emerging opportunities.

CBQ is a dominant player in the retail banking environment in Qatar. It issues approximately 50 per cent of all credit cards and enjoys over 90 per cent market share in the acquiring business. CBQ has established itself as a leading innovator in Qatar and indeed the Gulf region with many notable 'firsts to market'. In particular, it is regarded as a pioneer in the area of electronic banking. CBQ has the exclusive rights to the Diners Club franchise in many markets throughout the Middle East, giving it an important international focus through this affiliation, which is complemented by the Bank's links with other global financial institutions.

The Bank's ultimate objective is to become the preferred choice in Qatar for retail, investment and corporate banking services. The development of a diverse and sophisticated range of services is providing the solid platform from which to achieve this goal in the coming years.

More information can be obtained from the CBQ Call Centre by calling (+974) 4490000 and CBQ website: www.cbq.com.qa

Dallah Advertising Agency was established in 1981 to provide clients with a full range of marketing and communication services including advertising, marketing, public relations, market research, media planning and scheduling, event management, photography and videography and professional copywriting. The agency is part of the wider Dallah Group of Companies, which also incorporates E-Click Media Solutions, Dallah Outdoor, New Vision Visual Communications and Premadasa Colourscan Doha.

Mohammed Kadoumi is the Client Services Manager of Dallah Advertising Agency in Doha. He has experience in advertising, public relations and the media gained over a seven-year period in the markets of Jordan and Qatar.

The Middle East firm of **Ernst & Young** is a full-service professional organization offering a complete range of financial, taxation and business advice to entities investing and operating in Middle Eastern countries. Having been in the Middle East since 1923, the Middle East firm has over 800 staff and 15 offices located in 11 countries. Of the 57 partners resident in the Middle East, 30, including the Chairman, are Arab nationals. The Qatar practice conducts its activities through an office in Doha and has been practising in Qatar since 1952. The firm has the following divisions: audit and accounting, taxation and business advisory. The business advisory and tax practice in Qatar advises a large number of international companies and is the largest commercial advisory and tax consultancy practice in Qatar.

Finbarr Sexton is a Tax Partner in the Doha office of Ernst & Young. He is responsible for business and tax advisory services to a large range of international companies operating in Qatar. Finbarr is a member of the Middle East firm's Tax Steering Group and is the international tax correspondent for a number of international tax agencies. He has been resident in Qatar for 14 years and has been involved in both the evolution of the current Corporate Tax Law in Qatar and also impending changes to both the Commercial and Investment Laws in the State.

Hassan A AlKhater was the first registered Qatari lawyer to obtain a Master's degree in Law from a Western university. He is also the first Qatari to have worked for two international law firms, Trowers and Hamlins in Oman and Clyde & Co in Dubai. He was also Senior Legal Adviser and Company Secretary with Gulf Air, Bahrain. His main areas of practice are civil litigation, commercial litigation, shipping, oil and gas and construction.

Hassan A AlKhater Law Office concentrates on the representation of corporate clients, both inward-investing companies and established local companies that are carrying on business in Qatar, and advises on all aspects of commercial and civil laws, both contentious and non-contentious. It provides a full range of corporate and commercial legal services to its clients in connection with the acquisition, structuring, formation, financing and operation of investment vehicles and, in the case of contentious matters, arbitrations and proceedings before the Civil Court. The list of clients that the firm has advised includes ExxonMobil, Occidental Petroleum of Qatar Limited, Arco Qatar Inc, TotalFinaElf, Marubeni Corporation, Chevron, BP Amoco, HSBC Bank Middle East, Credit Suisse First Boston, Dresdner Kleinwort Benson, Standard Chartered Bank, Norsk Hydro, Gulf Agency, Alcatel, ABB, Interbeton and Schlumberger. The firm has acted also as adviser to the Embassies of the United States, Britain and Germany.

David Silver is a Solicitor who has practised in the Middle East for approximately 20 years. Formerly a partner with Clyde & Co in Dubai and London, he has worked in Qatar for more than five years and is the Honorary Legal Adviser to the British Ambassador. His main areas of practice are corporate law, project finance, oil and gas and commercial law.

InCite Marketing Research is a full-service market research agency with operations throughout the Arabian Peninsula. Established in 1994, the company's head office is in Bahrain and it has a subsidiary in the United Arab Emirates. With quantitative and qualitative research expertise, InCite conducts studies among consumers as well as business-to-business and industrial level.

Philip Keating was until early 2002 the Defence Attaché at the British Embassy in Doha.

Gordon MacKenzie has an extensive career in hotel management, particularly in the Middle East. His experience covers hotels in Sudan, Saudi Arabia, Jordan, Lebanon, the United Arab Emirates and Qatar. He is presently General Manager of the Ramada Hotel, Doha, where he has been for many years.

The **Philip Dew Consultancy Limited** was founded in 1982 to support local and international principals in the comprehensive development of their businesses in the Middle East. The basic services provided include: identification, investigation and evaluation of market opportunities; market research and feasibility studies; identification of partners, principals and associates; development of marketing and business strategies; and on-the-ground support and assistance to market entrants, including the provision of background and cultural information. To date, assignments have been fulfilled for over 250 companies and individuals.

The business is owned and managed by **Philip Dew**, who has been in the Middle East for over 30 years, is an Arabic speaker and who acted as consultant on *Doing Business with the UAE*, *Doing Business with Bahrain* and *Doing Business with Iran* prior to being involved as Consultant Editor on this book and *Doing Business with Oman*.

Philip Dew is based in Bahrain from where he covers the whole Middle East.

Qatar Industrial Development Bank (QIDB) is the government-owned specialized financial institution engaged in the identification, development, promotion and financing of industrial projects in Qatar.

Shaikh Hamad Nasser AlThani Ph.D. is the General Manager of Qatar Industrial Development Bank (QIDB). He has an MBA in Financial Planning from the University of Wales, and received his PhD in Industrial Project Management from the same university. At the time of joining the QIDB, Shaikh Hamad was Deputy Treasurer with Qatar Liquefied Gas Company Ltd. Prior to that, he held several key positions in the oil and gas industry.

Qatar Insurance Company is the oldest and largest national insurance company operating within Qatar. It was founded in 1964 with a substantial governmental shareholding. Today, the government continues to retain a share of the company. In 2000, the company received ISO 9000 accreditation as part of a drive to improve constantly the services to its clients.

From its foundation in 1964 with a capital of one million Indian rupees, the company has grown to a net worth approaching US$200 million. The company enjoys a Standard and Poor's Triple B rating.

Ian Sangster, Qatar Insurance Company's Assistant General Manager in charge of underwriting, first came to the Gulf in 1977. His career spans 36 years and his specific expertise lies in the energy and construction insurance fields. Before coming to Qatar he represented an international re-insurer throughout the Middle East.

Jeremy Williams OBE has spent more than 16 years in five Gulf locations: Sharjah, Dubai, Riyadh, Abu Dhabi and Bahrain. He was Defence, Naval, Military and Air Attaché in the British Embassies in Abu Dhabi and Bahrain. Jeremy Williams OBE has spent more than 16 years in five Gulf locations. His company, **Handshaikh Ltd**, offers bespoke on-site seminars in the UK, Gulf and USA that focus on the cross-cultural aspects of life and work in the Gulf. His business book *Don't they know it's Friday?* (Motivate Publishing, Dubai, now in its 3rd reprint) addresses the cross-cultural aspects of Westerners' experiences with Gulf Arabs. Handshaikh Ltd: UK: Tel. + 44 (0)1962 771699, Fax 01962 771814, Dubai: Tel.(+ 971 4) 3517624, Fax 3521033. Website: www.handshaikh.com; Email: mail@handshaikh.com.

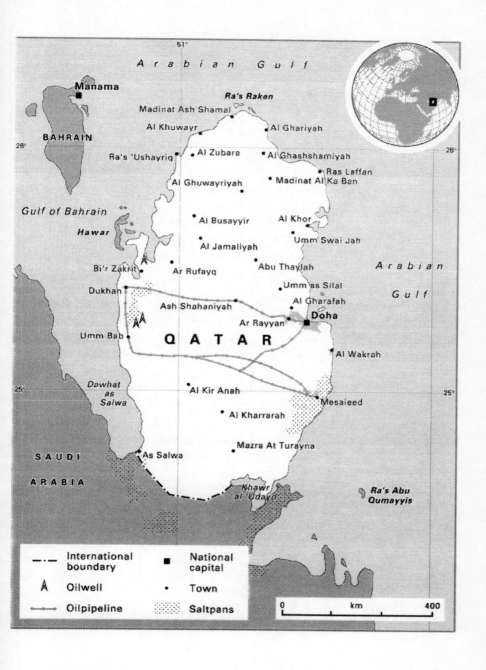

Map 1: Qatar and its Neighbours

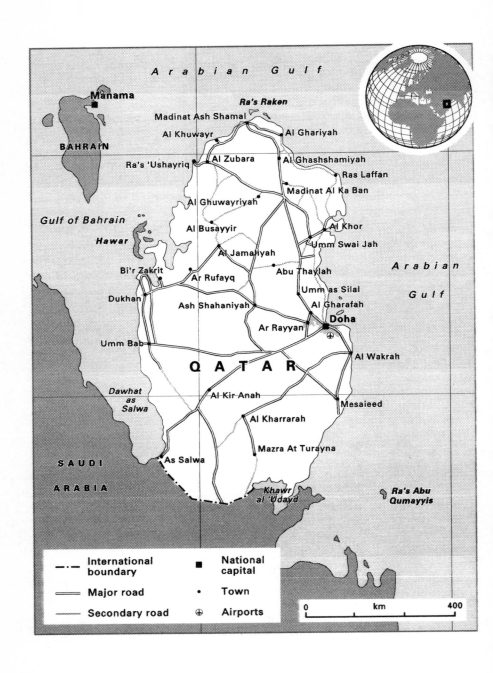

Map 2: The Infrastructure of Qatar

Part One

The Background to the Market

Geography and History

Philip Dew, Philip Dew Consultancy Limited, Bahrain

Geography

With a total land area of 11,437 square kilometres (4,416 square miles), Qatar comprises a peninsula, between 55 and 90 kilometres (34 and 56 miles) wide and some 160 kilometres (99 miles) in length, protruding from the Arabian mainland into the western extremities of the Arabian Gulf. To the west, Qatar is bordered by Saudi Arabia and to the south-east by the United Arab Emirates. The country's coastline extends 563 kilometres (350 miles) along its eastern, northern and western borders.

Overall, the country is low-lying with its highest point at Qurayn Abu AlBawl being just 103 metres (338 feet) above sea level. Primarily the country comprises stony, scrub desert with salt flats in a number of locations around the coast bordered in places by not insubstantial sand dunes. Offshore are a number of small islands and sand flats. There are resources of underground water but this is unsuitable for either agriculture or human consumption.

Qatar's climate is hot and humid in the summer months, with temperatures reaching 50°C between July and September and with the level of humidity attaining 90 per cent on occasion. Winter temperatures are equable at between 10°C and 20°C, due in part to infrequent rain showers of limited duration and averaging just 80 millimetres per year.

Qatar's population at the time of the 1997 census was 522,023, with an annual population growth of 3.6 per cent. More recent official estimates put the population substantially higher than the extrapolated figures might suggest. Some 60 per cent of the total population resides in Doha, the capital city, with the remainder spread throughout the peninsula in smaller towns and villages. Ras Laffan and the surrounding area in the north, the centre for the country's gas and allied industries, is fast becoming a major population centre.

History

Archaeological evidence suggests settlements existed in the area of today's Qatar as far back as 8,000 BC with strong evidence to indicate continued habitation since the fourth millennium BC. The name 'Qatara' is first mentioned in the writings of the Greek geographer, Ptolemy, in the second century CE, with the name 'Gattar' first appearing on a map produced by the Danish traveller Carsten Niebuhr in the 18th century CE.

The residents of Qatar became early adherents to the tenets of Islam in 628 CE, subsequently maintaining a close relationship with the caliphate, particularly during the Abbasid era in the 14th century CE, when the country experienced economic prosperity arising from the sale of high-quality local pearls to Baghdad.

Some 200 years later, in the 16th century CE, Qatar allied itself with the Ottoman Empire, which alliance lasted to varying extents until the second decade of the 20th century CE. At this time, the growth in neighbouring Saudi Arabia of Unitarianism, which tends to be known in the West as 'Wahhabism', allied to the defeat of the Ottomans in the eastern Saudi province of AlHasa in 1913, had a marked impact on Qatar as Ottoman influence commenced its decline.

At the onset of World War I, the Turks and the British, the latter of whom had for over 100 years maintained a strong influence in the Arabian Gulf, found themselves in opposition. With strong memories of an Ottoman invasion of their country in 1893, allied to the diminution of Ottoman influence in the region, the then Qatari ruler, Shaikh Abdullah bin Qasim AlThani, signed a Treaty of Protection with Britain in 1916 which, *inter alia*, recognized him as the independent ruler of Qatar.

Oil was first found in Qatar in 1939, but the start of World War II that same year caused all activities in this regard to be abandoned until 1949, at which time the country saw enhanced exploration and extraction activities, culminating in the first export of oil from the port of Dukhan the same year. Subsequently,

Qatar has become increasingly important as a major resource of natural gas, with proven reserves of 385 trillion cubic feet, the third largest known resource in the world.

Qatar became a fully independent state in 1971, with a total population estimated at that time of just 82,000. Since then, Qatar has been ruled by three members of the AlThani family, with the present Emir, Shaikh Hamad bin Khalifah AlThani having assumed power in 1995. His third son, Shaikh Jassim bin Hamad AlThani, has been appointed Crown Prince.

The Emir's role is governed by the provisional constitution adopted in 1970. He is supported by a Council of Ministers, which is appointed by Emiri Decree and is the supreme executive authority in the country. In 1972, Qatar became the first state in the region to have a Consultative (Advisory) Council, a body that today has 35 members, all of whom are appointed. Three years after its formation, this body was granted the right to summon individual ministers to discuss proposed legislation prior to its promulgation.

In 1999, a high-level, 32-member committee was formed to draft a permanent constitution for the country by 2002, integral to which, it has been suggested, will be the establishment of an elected parliament. A step in this direction occurred in 1999 when democratic elections were held for the 29 seats on the Central Municipal Council, an advisory body to the Ministry of Municipal Affairs and Agriculture. Women were allowed both to vote and to stand as candidates, a situation thought likely to prevail when parliamentary elections take place.

Qatar is a member of a number of international bodies, including the United Nations, the Arab League, OAPEC, OPEC and the GCC (Gulf Cooperation Council, a grouping that also includes Bahrain, Kuwait, Oman, Saudi Arabia and the United Arab Emirates).

1.2

The Economy

Philip Dew, Philip Dew Consultancy Limited, Bahrain

Introduction

Over the past 10 years, major changes have taken place in the structure of Qatar's economy. Having once been largely dependent on oil, which inevitably meant high vulnerability to fluctuations in its price on world markets, Qatar has sought to diversify its economy by giving greater attention to its vast gas reserves and to developing major, interrelated downstream industries.

In 2000, Qatar's GDP grew at an annual rate of 12 per cent, due in large part to increased oil reserves and a sharp increase in natural gas exports. In 2001, the rate of growth was estimated at approximately 6 per cent, a level that analysts suggest could be sustained at least during 2002 and perhaps in future years. The figure for the coming years is predicated on the basis of expected increases in the rates of production and export of natural gas.

A direct result of the moves towards economic diversification has been a substantial increase in investment in major projects, particularly those related to liquefied natural gas (LNG) and its export but also to new and enlarged petrochemical facilities (see Chapter 1.3). Further investment is anticipated in the years to come to ensure derivation of the maximum benefit from the country's resources.

In the short term, however, Qatar is perceived likely to face a testing time in servicing its debt, which equates to some 90 per cent of GDP. Progressively, this situation is expected to ease as the revenues from the investments begin to flow and to increase in value and the level of new investment reduces.

This situation means that in the short-to-medium term only a limited proportion of these anticipated revenues are likely to find their way into the domestic economy – as a majority of all funding emanated from overseas and many of the contracts for consultancy, engineering, procurement and implementation of the infrastructure and the facilities themselves were let to foreign companies. Estimates differ as to when the local economy will begin to derive meaningful benefit from the projects, but analysts have suggested a time-frame between 2002 and 2005. In part, this will depend on what further investment is undertaken and the level of revenue that can be derived from existing facilities, but consensus would suggest the latter date to be more accurate.

Although Qatar is becoming increasingly dependent on gas, oil production also remains important and is likely to rise from the current level of 608,500 barrels per day (Source: OPEC) to some 900,000 barrels per day in 2004 – an anticipated increase that will of course be impacted by the global economic environment and OPEC agreements over the defined period. That said, and as indicated earlier, it will be some years before the real benefits of the gas programme are felt and in the meantime, therefore, oil income will remain an important revenue source for the government.

Gross domestic product (GDP)

The breakdown of GDP by sector over the period 1996–2000 can be seen in Table 1.2.1.

Year-on-year GDP growth between 1996 and 2000 averaged 12.3 per cent, albeit 1998 saw a marked fall in GDP as evidenced in Table 1.2.2.

The oil and gas sector clearly remains by far the major contributor to GDP, accounting for almost 50 per cent of the estimated figures for 2000. The balance of GDP was made up of 'other services' (which includes government, social and household services, import tariffs and imputed bank service charges) 16 per cent; manufacturing 8 per cent; trade, restaurants and hotels 7 per cent; transport and communications 5 per cent; and construction 4 per cent.

Based on the estimated figures and a population of 580,000 (also an estimate), GDP per capita in 2000 amounted to US$25,234,

Table 1.2.1 GDP by sector (QR million)

Economic sector	1996	1997	1998	1999	2000
Oil sector	12,773	17,386	14,025	19,950	26,435
Non-oil sector	20,203	23,738	24,049	24,447	26,841
Breakdown (non-oil)					
Agriculture and fisheries	290	290	299	260	250
Manufacturing	2,499	3,417	3,425	3,250	4,200
Utilities	427	482	520	640	675
Construction	2,268	2,873	2,880	2,180	2,300
Trade, hotels and restaurants	2,544	2,762	2,785	3,210	3,690
Transportation and communications	1,223	1,451	1,535	1,952	2,520
Finance, insurance and real estate	3,423	3,969	3,990	4,619	4,900
Other services	7,529	8,494	8,615	8,336	8,306
Total	**32,976**	**41,124**	**38,074**	**44,397**	**53,276**

Sources: Qatar Central Bank, The Planning Council and Qatar National Bank (2000, estimate).

an increase of nearly 12 per cent over a year earlier. This figure is one of the highest globally.

Balance and direction of trade

Over the five-year period 1995–1999 inclusive, Qatar maintained a positive balance of trade as indicated in Table 1.2.3.
Between 1997 and 1999, the surplus on trade grew by in excess of 150 per cent, due to an overall increase of exports of 38 per cent, while import growth amounted to just 5 per cent over the same period.

Table 1.2.2 Total GDP (US$ million)

1996	1997	1998	1999	2000
9,059	11,298	10,459	12,197	14,636

Sources: Qatar Central Bank 1996–1999, Qatar National Bank (2000, estimate).

Table 1.2.3 Balance of trade (QR million)

Item	1995	1996	1997	1998	1999
Export	12,948	13,952	14,036	18,311	19,385
Import	11,008	9,406	10,893	11,177	11,457
Balance	**1,940**	**4,546**	**3,143**	**7,134**	**7,928**

Source: Qatar Central Bank and other private sources.

Qatar's main trading partners have historically been the United States, Japan, the United Kingdom, Germany, France and Italy (with many imports passing through the United Arab Emirates en route to Qatar), but, more recently, long-term agreements have been signed for sales of natural gas with other trading partners such as India and South Korea, as well as with Japan, thereby increasing these countries' importance in bilateral trade.

The future

Indications are that Qatar's economic future is secure despite being vulnerable to changes in world oil prices, which inevitably also impact on gas prices, and in global economic circumstances. Integral to this are likely to be enhanced budgetary controls to ensure derivation of the maximum benefit by the domestic economy from the anticipated increased revenue flows.

1.3

Oil, Gas and Petrochemicals

Philip Dew, Philip Dew Consultancy Limited, Bahrain

Oil

Qatar has proven, recoverable oil reserves amounting to 3.7 billion barrels (OPEC figure) located in seven fields, of which Dukhan, along the country's west coast, is the largest. The other six fields are all offshore.

In mid-2001, Qatar was producing an average of 700,000 barrels per day of crude oil, a figure that could increase to in excess of one million barrels per day as development of the sector proceeds. From September 2001, Qatar's OPEC crude production was set at 601,000 barrels per day.

Since 1995, a number of policies have been initiated by the government to seek to increase oil production while increasing exploration, specifically to seek further resources that are less expensive to recover, and extending the life of existing fields through the use of advanced recovery systems. Integral to this activity have been improved exploration and production contracts intended to encourage greater foreign investment in the sector. The success of this policy is indicated by the involvement in recent years of companies such as Chevron, MOL of Hungary, Arco (now part of BP Amoco), Wintershall, Pennzoil, Gulfstream Resources (now owned by Anadarko of the United States) and BG International (formerly British Gas). Other operating companies, some of which have been involved in Qatar for many years, include TotalFinaElf (through Elf Aquitaine Qatar), Maersk Oil Qatar and Occidental Petroleum.

The latest Qatari offshore field to come on-stream is AlKhalij, which has a capability of producing up to 60,000 barrels per day of medium sweet crude. Other fields now in production include Maydan Mahzam (50,000 barrels per day), Bulttanine (70,000 barrels per day, after being much higher in earlier years), Id alShargi North Dome (approximately 100,000 barrels per day) and AlShaheen (150,000 barrels per day currently, but being developed to ultimately produce 200,000 barrels per day).

Downstream, Qatar Petroleum's Directorate of Refineries (formerly National Oil Distribution Company, NODCO) recently upgraded the refinery at Mesaieed (Um Said) to permit throughput of 137,000 barrels per day. The upgrading improved the economics of the refinery while enhancing compliance with international environmental standards.

Gas

Qatar's known gas resources are the third largest in the world behind Russia and Iran, at 385 trillion cubic feet. A substantial majority of this gas is to be found in the North Field, which is reported to contain some 380 trillion cubic feet of gas, of which some 240 trillion cubic feet is regarded as recoverable. These figures make this the largest single non-associated gas field in the world. The remaining reserves are to be found as associated gas in the country's oilfields.

In recent years, Qatar has recognized that its national economic future lies in the maximum exploitation of its gas resources and, to this end, two major companies were formed to produce and export LNG – namely, Qatar Liquefied Gas Company (Qatargas) and RasGas Company (RasGas). Qatar Petroleum (QP) has a major stake in both of these companies, as do international concerns such as ExxonMobil (in both entities), TotalFinaElf, Mitsui and Marubeni in (Qatargas) and Itochu Corporation, Nissho Iwai Corporation and Korean Gas Corporation (in Rasgas).

Exports of LNG have been targeted at the Far East, mainly Japan and Korea, although India is thought likely to become an important client in the coming years.

A most important project with regard to Qatar's gas is the Dolphin Project, which aims to install a gas pipeline linking Qatar with the United Arab Emirates (the lead country), Oman and, possibly, Pakistan. The project aims to supply some 730 billion cubic feet of gas per year from the North Field to Abu Dhabi, starting in 2005. Bahrain and Kuwait also have agreements with Qatar for the supply of gas and a gas pipeline direct to Pakistan has also been under consideration.

In addition, two gas-to-liquid projects, converting methane gas into environmentally friendly middle distillates, are under consideration – one with Sasol Synfuels International of South Africa (34,000 barrels per day) and the other with ExxonMobil (80,000 barrels per day).

Petrochemicals

Taking advantage of its immense supply of feedstock, Qatar – and specifically QP – has moved rapidly ahead to produce added value products by establishing facilities capable of producing an array of petrochemicals including ethylene, polyethylene, ammonia, urea, polythene, methanol, ethylene dichloride and vinyl chloride monomer. Details of individual companies involved in this sector are outlined below.

According to sources in Qatar, a number of other petrochemical projects are under consideration for implementation in the coming years. These include an ethane cracker; another plant to produce methanol; a new ammonia and urea plant; a facility to produce high- and low-density polyethylene, ethylene oxide glycol, propylene and polypropylene; an aromatics complex; a further polypropylene plant; two more methanol trains; and a plant to produce toluene di-isocyanate.

Local companies involved in oil, gas and petrochemicals

Qatar Petroleum (QP)

Qatar Petroleum (QP), which replaced the Qatar General Petroleum Corporation (QGPC) in January 2001, is the state-owned company charged with responsibility for all aspects of the oil and gas industries both in Qatar and overseas – from exploration and drilling through to the derivatives and by-products of oil and gas. In addition, QP is responsible for the three industrial cities at Ras Laffan, where the country's LNG export terminal is situated; Dukhan (the centre of onshore oil operations); and Mesaieed (the location of the country's oil refinery).

Qatar Petrochemical Company (QAPCO)

Qatar Petrochemical Company (QAPCO), 80 per cent owned by QP, produces ethylene, low-density polyethylene (LDPE) and prilled sulphur. Production in 2000 amounted to 525,000 tonnes of ethylene; 360,000 tonnes of LDPE; and 70,000 tonnes of prilled sulphur. Much of the company's ethylene production is utilized in-house to produce LDPE, but is also sold locally as feedstock for Qatar Vinyl Company (QVC) and exported to India, Indonesia and other Asian countries. Expansion and de-bottlenecking of QAPCO's facilities can be anticipated during 2002. QAPCO's foreign partners are AtoFina of France and Enichem of Italy.

Qatar Fertilizer Company (QAFCO)

Qatar Fertilizer Company (QAFCO), 75 per cent owned by QP, produces ammonia and urea, all of which is exported to some 25 countries worldwide, with India being the lead market. Following on from a number of expansion projects since first being formed in 1974, QAFCO today has a productive capacity of 1.3 million tonnes per year of ammonia and 1.6 million tonnes per year of urea from three integrated plants. A fourth plant is under construction for commissioning in 2004, with a capacity of 700,000 tonnes per year of ammonia and 1.12 million tonnes per year of urea, when QAFCO expects to become the world's largest single-site ammonia and urea producer in the world. The foreign partner in QAFCO is Norsk Hydro.

Qatar Liquefied Gas Company Ltd (Qatargas)

Qatar Liquefied Gas Company Ltd (Qatargas) was Qatar's first LNG company, which today has a capacity of nearly 7 million tonnes per year, but which will, in 2005, be capable of producing 9 million tonnes per year. Consideration is also being given to a fourth LNG train capable of producing 4.8 million tonnes per year. Actual production in 2001 was 7.4 million tonnes. Qatar Petroleum owns 65 per cent of QatarGas, with its partners TotalFinaElf, ExxonMobil, Mitsui and Marubeni holding the balance. Liquefied natural gas from the company's facilities is mainly exported on long-term contracts to Japan and Spain, although a number of short-term sales have also been agreed. QatarGas was the first LNG company worldwide to hold both ISO 9002 and 14001 – the former of which was upgraded in 2001 to ISO 9001:2000.

Ras Laffan Liquefied Natural Gas Company Ltd (RasGas)

Sixty-five per cent owned by QP along with ExxonMobil, Itochu Corporation and Nissho Iwai, RasGas has a nominal production capacity of 6.6 million tonnes per year from two trains. Major long-term export contracts have been signed with companies in Korea, India, Taiwan and Italy. Two further trains are under consideration, which would boost productive capacity to 16 million tonnes per year, as is a helium plant, which would take advantage of the helium available in the LNG process from both RasGas and QatarGas.

Qatar Chemical Company (Q-Chem)

Qatar Chemical Company (Q-Chem) is a joint venture between QP (51 per cent) and Chevron Philips Chemical Qatar to produce 500,000 tonnes per year of ethylene; a 462,000 tonnes-per-year polyethylene plant, of which 273,000 tonnes high-density poly-ethylene (HDPE) and 189,000 tonnes LDPE; and 47,000 tonnes hexene-1. Production is scheduled to start in mid-to-late 2002.

Qatar Fuel Additives Company (QAFAC)

Fifty per cent owned by QP, QAFAC's plant is designed to produce 825,000 tonnes per year of AA-grade methanol, of which approximately one-quarter is to be used as feedstock to produce 610,000 tonnes per year of methyl tertiary-butyl ether (MTBE). The foreign partners are Chinese Petroleum Corporation, Lee Chang Yung Chemical Industry Corporation and International Octane Limited.

Qatar Vinyl Company (QVC)

Production at Qatar Vinyl Company (QVC) commenced in May 2001. Fifty-one per cent owned by QP, this ethylene dichloride (175,000 tonnes per year), vinyl chloride monomer (230,000 tonnes per year) and caustic soda (290,000 tonnes per year) plant will export much of its production to South-East Asia. Expansion of the existing plant is already under consideration with the possibility of a polyvinyl chloride (PVC) facility also being added.

Other investments

In addition to the above, QP has a number of investments including Gulf Helicopters (100 per cent), which provides worker transportation offshore; Qatar Plastic Products Company (26.6 per cent indirectly through QAPCO), which produces heavy-duty plastic bags; and Qatar Nitrogen Company (50 per cent), which produces both gas and liquid nitrogen.

1.4

Commercial Environment

David Chaddock, Management Consultant

Introduction

Qatar has a split personality with respect to its methods and attitudes to doing business. On the one hand, the country is full of optimism and forward thinking. On the other, it remains extremely conservative with respect to change.

As a result, the commercial community and environment within which one must work varies from the frankly archaic to the modern. New entrants to the market should be prepared for a lengthy wait while their proposals are considered and their serious intent tested. In the traditional style of the Middle East, personal introductions, recommendations and longevity play extremely important roles.

The choice of partner is also of paramount importance. The commercial world is even more a village community in Qatar than elsewhere. Business is owned by and revolves around the major families and tribes. Personalities, personal attitudes and the extent of connections will make or break a venture. To add to the complexity, these can be simple and current or deeply layered over several generations. They will seldom be apparent.

For success, an understanding of the history of the country and the roles that the various families and tribes have had in its development during the short life of the modern State of Qatar is of paramount importance. This is in addition, of course, to accounting for all the usual advice about ensuring that the potential partner is even capable of cooperating in the manner required.

Public sector

Privatization versus reality

While 'privatization' remains the goal and is a key word in the government's plans and policies, it is correct to say that all primary industry remains in government hands. Even where privatization has occurred, a cursory look at the shareholders makes it clear that it is the first step in that direction rather than a reality. This includes the oil and gas industry, telecommunications, medical and welfare, and power and water.

The moves allowed some of these sectors and businesses to be more open and independent of direct government control, but the mindset of employees in changing from a 'civil service' to a market-led, quality-based, fit-for-the-purpose approach is difficult. Traditional values and systems come back and bite unless people have been retrained or, as has occurred in some instances, changed.

Oil and gas

The oil and gas sector is a *mélange* of joint venture companies with a majority ownership by the government through Qatar Petroleum (QP; formerly Qatar General Petroleum Corporation, QGPC). While generally following the QP system, each industrial company has its own ethos, which is usually generated by that of the principal foreign partners.

Telecommunications

Although privatized, Qatar Telecommunications Company (Q-Tel) remains a monopoly and covers all aspects of both terrestrial and mobile telephone, telephony and Internet services. Obtaining service and doing business with Q-Tel must be considered with this fact in mind.

Medical and welfare

Medical care, which is free for citizens and residents, is provided through government clinics and the Hamad Medical Centre. Additional new private hospitals and clinics are under construction. Some are targeted at specific groups or sectors of the population, while others are more general in their aim. Expanding opportunities exist to build and service the construction of this growth area.

Power and water

The power and water sector has gone through a major reorganization from a single government ministry (Ministry of Electricity and Water, MEW) covering all aspects of ownership, production, transmission and distribution of electricity and water to the consumer, to a semi-privatized operation, Qatar General Electricity and Water Corporation (QGEWC), which has a clear split between generation and transmission, and distribution to the consumer. The supply of generating plant is now targeted for private initiative, with control and part-ownership remaining with QGEWC (or 'Kahrabaa' as it is more generally known). A private company, Qatar Electricity & Water Company (QEWC) has been established to handle operations and maintenance of primary power plant, as a contractor to Kahrabaa. Distribution remains within the full control of Kahrabaa. Recently, the first contract was let for a private power plant in Ras Laffan and the next phase of the electricity transmission network has been launched.

Ministries

In dealing with government ministries there has been no appreciable change in approach. In general, the appropriate individuals are accessible for promotion of products and services and to and from whom to gain information on planning. For business contracts, however, public tenders issued through the Central Tenders Committee continue to rule the day. The same public tender system applies to quasi-governmental businesses, such as the Qatar National Hotels Company, which owns the majority of first-class hotels and leisure properties in Qatar. That said, there is always the possibility for direct purchases from nominated suppliers, as circumstances and needs dictate.

Private sector

Manufacturing

Since accession to power by the current Emir, private sector confidence and willingness to invest in the country has grown substantially. While manufacturing industries to support the growing mainstream oil- and gas-related industrial plants have grown significantly along with the new investment in those areas, they are not yet in the abundance seen in neighbouring countries. There remain many opportunities in both the support and light manufacturing industries. The policy to promote industrial development that utilizes the products from its mineral wealth remains a cornerstone of the government's plans. Private initiatives are welcomed for foreign or joint investment in these fields.

Contracting

Contracting is a difficult market. Local companies dominate and price levels are extremely competitive. The accent on quality is yet to be fully understood. In private projects particularly, the personal interests and preferences mentioned in the opening paragraphs come into full play along with a generally conservative approach summarized by 'better the devil you know than the devil you don't'. New entrants must be prepared to struggle against this. Reputation outside the country is not always a sure counter, particularly if the experience is also outside the region. Payments to, and therefore from, main contractors is variable, depending on the client. The wise contractor, or subcontractor, will research and understand the client, his consultant and any other advisers before entering into any marginal or time-constrained project.

To prevent negative surprises, local availability and/or accessibility of critical requirements such as basic support services, equipment, materials and manpower should be thoroughly researched by new entrants. Currently, manpower numbers are strictly controlled on a nationality basis, and sources of materials and services continue to grow to meet demand.

Trading

Attitudes in trading companies by and large remain traditional. Wholesale and resale companies tend to carry the minimum stock of fast-moving items, with the balance 'in store'. Often the location of the 'store' is the shops and warehouses of stocking distributors in neighbouring countries from where larger volumes can readily be purchased. Product knowledge and advice is often limited, as is any depth in staff.

The 'indent agent' approach remains the dominant method of trading in engineered and industrial products. The local agents prefer to rely on the supplier to provide expertise and thereby cover for responsibility for suitability of application and installed performance.

Hospitality

The hospitality industry, together with sport, continues to be a major growth area. In addition to the existing international sports events hosted by Qatar (eg tennis, athletics, golf, football, volleyball, squash, handball), the selection of Qatar as host for the Asian Games in 2006 has called for a rapid increase in the construction of additional world-class sports facilities and all areas of the hospitality industry. There is currently a mini-boom in the construction of new hotels, which is expected to continue unabated for the next few years. On the back of these are additional restaurants and leisure activity centres. All require specialized design, equipment and services, which in themselves are creating a wealth of new opportunity in supply and local fabrication/assembly and manufacture.

Retail

Retail activities are growing fast. The expectation of large numbers of shoppers from both the resident and transient populations have spawned a number of new shopping complexes, with more under construction or at the planning stage. It is to be noted that the modern malls are contrasted with the traditional 'souks' and the mentality of both shoppers and shop-owners to suit. The bulk of the population of shoppers remains very much host-nation national, other Arabs from the Gulf and wider Middle East and individuals from the Indian Sub-Continent. With recent developments, the style of shopping and the demands of consumers have visibly changed, with a far wider variety of product now available. However, the supply chain system remains the same and to achieve success it is necessary to work with a good local distributor.

Advertising

Neither advertising nor publishing in Qatar can be considered major industries. Both are hamstrung by the size of the markets and the perception by advertisers of what advertising is and does and therefore attitude towards cost and benefit. Most advertising is still carried out in daily newspapers and on billboards. Both radio and television have made attempts to promote themselves as valid alternatives, but seemingly with little success. There are a growing number of subject-specific periodicals produced locally or produced in neighbouring countries and targeting the Qatari market. Rates for advertising in all media tend to be extremely attractive in comparison to rates found elsewhere in the Gulf.

1.5

Tourism, Trade Fairs, Exhibitions and Conferences

Gordon MacKenzie, General Manager, Ramada Hotel, Doha, Qatar

Introduction

Qatar has the potential and strength to ensure a successful future for tourism and as a destination for business people attending trade fairs, exhibitions and conferences. Integral to this, every encouragement has been given to the private sector to participate either independently or together with various government agencies in providing a comprehensive infrastructure for both participants and visitors to enjoy their stay, while partaking of Qatar's warm hospitality.

Climate

Qatar has a desert climate where summers are long and hot but winters start in November and last until March and the climate is cooler (albeit very little rain falls during this period). A major advantage is that the average humidity is lower in Qatar than it tends to be in its Arabian Gulf neighbours.

Heritage and culture

Doha is the only Gulf capital that can claim to have preserved almost all historical buildings, with many recent buildings incorporating traditional Arabic architecture but in a contemporary manner.

Among the most significant cultural features in Doha is the National Museum, which won the Aga Khan International Award for the excellence of its renovation as a surviving masterpiece of traditional Qatari architecture. This former palace of the ruling AlThani family now houses a wide collection of historical and traditional artefacts from Qatar and the Arabian Gulf region, plus a gallery depicting the country's development since the discovery of oil in 1939.

Particular aspects of national heritage that can also be witnessed include the ancient art of falconry and hunting with saluki dogs.

Areas of interest

Beaches and sea

Beaches spread from north to south of the peninsula, with some hotels offering their own privately developed beaches for a more relaxed ambience.

The Inland Sea – a natural sea incursion near the Saudi border – is a largely untouched part of Qatar, with the most staggering, uninterrupted views of the wide, expansive desert and hosting the most spectacular and impressive sand dunes in the country, all set around a bay and towering some 40 metres towards the sky.

Desert

Qatar offers a combination of two traditions – one tied to the sea and the other to the desert – thus ensuring a unique environment for visitors to the country.

Sand dunes are a great attraction for both visitors and locals alike as they are ideal for both skiing and for driving across on safari. Four-wheel drive vehicles are essential, particularly for weekend drives into the desert, with overnight camping and desert barbecues being very popular events. During such journeys, travellers can still witness the Bedouin lifestyle and the small villages and their people dotted around the peninsula.

Oryx and camel farms

Qatar has taken pride in saving the rare Arabian Oryx, which is a protected species in the country, having at one time been considered virtually extinct. There is now a large and healthy herd of Oryx kept on a private estate near Shahaniya and, although it is necessary to obtain a permit to visit, a number of local tour companies do arrange trips.

Camel-breeding farms are found throughout the country, and desert safari packages will usually include a visit to one.

Corniche

Doha's beautiful corniche is one of the finest in the Middle East. Stretching for seven kilometres around a delightful bay, it is popular with both locals and tourists – be they those who are seeking to get fit or those who just want to take a gentle stroll and admire the scenery while breathing in the fresh sea air.

Al Shaqab Stud

Owned by the Emir, Shaikh Hamad bin Khalifa AlThani, this extensive stud farm has gained a worldwide reputation for its many champion horses, which include Imperial Phanilla, the world champion and Qatar champion mare in 1994.

Camel races

Camel races are often held at the main racetrack at Shahaniya. There is a large spectator stand, but most locals choose to follow the race in vehicles, adding to the excitement of the event.

Palm Tree Island

A true oasis in the middle of the sea, Palm Tree Island, 25,000 square metres in area, is covered with palm trees surrounded by beaches offering many water sport activities. The island also has a restaurant which serves a range of gastronomical delights to suit all tastes. Visitors to the island – and particularly children – can enjoy pony rides, picnics, sports, a play area and pleasantly laid-out walkways. The journey to the island by traditional dhow adds to the experience.

Doha Golf Club

Doha Golf Club is located eight kilometres from the city centre and business district of Doha. The club is considered the newest and most prestigious in the Middle East region. One of the world's leading golf course architects, Peter Harradine, has created an 18-hole par 72 championship course measuring 7,312 yards (6,686 metres) as well as a golf academy with its own nine-hole course overlooking the West Bay Lagoon.

The championship course has eight artificial lakes and is surrounded by 10,000 different species of trees, plants and shrubs, and provides an exciting challenge for golfers of every standard. The academy course is the perfect location for the less experienced.

Doha Zoo

Doha's municipal zoo is situated on the outskirts of Doha, approximately 30 minutes' drive from the town centre. There are plenty of shaded viewing areas from which to watch a comprehensive array of animals, insects and reptiles indigenous to Qatar, as well as from other parts of the world. An extensive play area is available for children.

Doha Fort

Also known as the AlKoot Fort, Doha Fort is Moorish in style and is a reminder of Turkish occupation during the 19th century. It is located at the corner of Jassim bin Mohammed and AlQalaa Streets, near the old souk area of downtown Doha.

AlZubara Fort

AlZubara Fort was built during the reign of Shaikh Abdullah bin Qasim AlThani in 1938 as a border police post. A small four-bastion structure around a courtyard, it was used by the military until well into the 1980s. Two kilometres beyond the fort area lie the ruins of various other coastal fortifications, near to which are a number of deserted fishing villages.

Sports and leisure

Qatar is home to many indoor and outdoor games, and sports clubs abound. Football is the most popular sport and Qatar plays host to many tournaments throughout the year. Billiards and snooker are very popular among the younger generation, as is swimming, with pools to be found all over the country. Water skiing is readily available at all resort hotels and on Palm Tree Island.

Tennis, squash, yacht racing and motor rallying, among other sports, all take place in the country, and many international events are hosted. Examples include the Qatar ExxonMobil ATP Tournament and the TotalFinaElf Women's Tournament, which attract top players in the world of tennis; the Equestrian Desert Marathon, an endurance horse race very popular among Gulf nationals; the Qatar International Rally, a part of the FIA Middle East Rally calendar; a World Squash Tournament; a World Skeet Tournament (skeet shooting); the Qatar International Sailing Regatta, open to local, regional and international competition; and, in 2002 for the first time, the Asia Pacific Laser Championships.

Qatar intends to become the Gulf's major sporting destination and to this end has won the right to stage the prestigious 2006 Asian Games. Plans are now being drafted for the hosting of this important event at which over 6,000 participants, spectators and guests are expected to attend.

Trade fairs, exhibitions and conferences

For many years, Doha has hosted trade fairs and exhibitions, be they thematic or specific to a given country. Doha has a modern exhibition centre but many exhibitions are also held in the major hotels. The majority of events take place during the cooler months of the year and include book fairs; environmental exhibitions; national trade shows, including the annual British Week; an international defence and security equipment show; educational exhibitions; fashion shows; and hotel equipment and food salons. Small though the local economy may be, these events attract worldwide participation and visitors from throughout the region.

Recently, Qatar has also hosted the latest round of World Trade Organization (WTO) meetings, in addition to high-level regional conferences attended by senior government representatives from within the Gulf and wider Arab World. Business conferences, including those organized by the Gulf Organization for Industrial Consulting, based in Doha, have ensured numerous visitors from the commercial sector seeking to develop their businesses around the region as well as in Qatar itself. As the country develops its facilities further, so increasing numbers of exhibitions, trade fairs and conferences will be drawn to the favourable environment that the government has created.

New developments

Qatar is wholly intent on becoming a popular tourist destination. As a result, a number of measures have been taken to pave the way for what is hoped will be a major influx of visitors:

● The recent creation of the Qatar Tourism Authority is a step forward and signifies the country's commitment towards inbound tourism.

● Qatar Airways has started visa-on-arrival arrangements, which make it more convenient for visitors to plan and organize their trips into the country.

● Doha International Airport has enjoyed a multi-million dollar refurbishment and improvement programme. Completion of the project has doubled the size of the original airport terminal buildings, which now have 14 gates. The immigration system has also been improved by utilizing the latest computer networks between the airport and the immigration and passport office.

● Over the coming years, the hospitality industry is expected to witness significant expansion. The Ritz Carlton, a luxury hotel, resort and spa, was opened on the West Bay Lagoon overlooking the Arabian Gulf in 2001, as was the Hotel Intercontinental. The Four Seasons Hotel project began implementation in 2001; a Holiday Inn is expected to open before the end of 2002; and Movenpick Hotels have gained a presence in the country under the umbrella of Qatar National Hotels. However, these will provide only a few of the many hotels and apartments which are expected to be added to Doha's hospitality portfolio in the coming months and years.

● Large and modern shopping centres are now an integral part of Doha's scenery. The Middle East's largest shopping complex,

City Centre Doha, opened in 2001, and together with Landmark, The Mall, Salam Plaza and The Centre provides a wide variety of household goods, ladies and gentlemen's fashions and accessories as well as branded perfumes and cosmetics.

● Modern cinemas are now widely found either individually or as part of one of the modern shopping complexes. They feature the latest English-language films as well as those in Arabic, Hindi and Urdu.

Conclusion

Qatar is increasingly becoming a broadly based destination for business travellers and tourists alike. As more facilities are constructed, so the country anticipates attracting more events to its shores, which will inevitably ensure increased employment for Qataris and a more diverse economic base.

Part Two

Establishing a Business in Qatar

Business Structures

David Silver, Solicitor, Hassan A AlKhater Law Office, Doha, Qatar

Introduction

Qatari law recognizes a number of possible business structures. However, few of them are available to foreign investors and this chapter will therefore focus only on those that can be used by foreign investors.

The investment of foreign capital in economic activity in Qatar is governed by the Foreign Investment Law, Law No. 13 of 2000, which establishes the general rule that such investment, where permitted, must be through a company incorporated in Qatar in which a minimum of 51 per cent of the capital is owned by one or more Qataris, whether natural or juristic. There are, however, two principal exceptions to this rule. The first is that a foreign entity undertaking a major contract may apply to the Minister of Economy and Commerce for an exemption from the Foreign Investment Law on the grounds that the performance of the contract in respect of which the application is made will result in a service for the public benefit. If granted, the exemption permits registration of the foreign entity in Qatar for the purpose only of carrying out the specific contract in respect of which the exemption is given. It does not permit the foreign entity to carry on any other business in Qatar. The second exception is that, in the case of a project to be established for any one or more of a number of defined purposes, the Minister may, at his discretion, permit the increase of the foreign equity participation in the project up to full foreign ownership. However, the Law expressly excludes foreign investment in the fields of banking, insurance, commercial agency and trading in real estate.

Types of business structure

The two most common forms of joint venture vehicle are the 'hidden' joint venture and the company with limited liability (WLL).

Hidden joint ventures

'Hidden' joint ventures are an agreement entered into between the foreign investor and a Qatari entity registered for the purpose of carrying on business of the nature that the foreign investor wishes to pursue. Such joint ventures are expressly precluded from carrying on those businesses that the Foreign Investment Law reserves solely for Qataris. A third party dealing with the joint venture vehicle will be deemed to have dealt with the Qatari entity and not with the foreign investor, unless the foreign investor has undertaken a specific act which brings the existence of the joint venture to the attention of the third party. Consequently, any claims will be made against the Qatari entity, leaving the Qatari entity to seek whatever recourse to which it may be entitled from the foreign investor.

There are a number of disadvantages to such joint ventures. These include the fact that the business must be conducted in the name of the Qatari entity and not in the name of the foreign investor. The business is wholly owned by the Qatari entity and the bank accounts through which the joint venture operates are the bank accounts of the Qatari entity. The employees designated by the foreign investor to work in the joint venture become employees of the Qatari entity; in the event of a dispute, those employees can be dismissed and may be prevented from working for any competing business in Qatar for a period of two years.

Companies with limited liability

Companies with limited liability (WLL) are incorporated pursuant to Chapter 4 of the Commercial Companies Law, Law No. 11 of 1981. Such companies have their own legal personality. They do not issue shares in their capital and the parties to the constitutive contract (equivalent to the memorandum and articles of association) are known as partners, rather than shareholders. Each partner owns a portion of the capital of the WLL. Each such portion carries a proportionate right to vote in the general assembly of the company, to receive a share of the profits of the company, if any, and a share in any surplus or deficit resulting from a liquidation of the company. Each such portion is capable of being sold or, in the case of a partner who is a natural person, of being transferred to his heirs on his death.

A limited liability company is capable of contracting in its own right, owning its own assets, opening and operating bank accounts and conferring limited liability upon its partners. Although in theory there is no obligation on the founder of a WLL to do so, in practice the department responsible for registration of companies will insist on the adoption of that department's standard form of constitutive contract. Any departure from the standard form must be approved by the department, which is reluctant to accept any changes.

Joint stock companies

A further business structure is available in the case of joint ventures entered into with the government or with corporations wholly owned by the government. This is a joint-stock company incorporated under the provisions of Article 90 of the Commercial Companies Law. Article 90 permits the government to establish a joint-stock company by itself or with one or more foreign nationals. Such companies will be exempt from the Commercial Companies Law to the extent that the Commercial Companies Law conflicts with the provisions of the memorandum and articles of association of the company.

2.2

Industrialization: Small and Medium-sized Industries (SMIs)

Classification of SMIs

Promotion of small and medium-sized industries (SMIs) is considered one of the most essential activities of the Qatari government in achieving comprehensive economic development, as well as being a mechanism that helps to achieve the horizontal and vertical integration of the industrial sector.

There are no clear-cut international definitions and dividing lines between small and medium-sized industry. One way to differentiate between the two is according to the size of invested capital. Such a criterion is more or less a reflection of the real situation in Qatar.

● Small industries: capital invested between QR250,000 and QR5 million (between US$68,680 and US$1.37 million).

● Medium-sized industries: capital invested between QR5 million and QR20 million (between US$1.37 million and US$5.49 million).

Accordingly, the total number of existing medium-sized industries in Qatar is 50 and small industries 264. Total capital employed in small industries by the end of 2000 was QR461.8 million (US$126.9 million) and in medium-sized industries QR524 million (US$144.1 million) – an overall total of QR1.085 billion (US$298 million). The total capital in the entire manufacturing industries at the same date was QR13.5 billion (US$3.7 billion). Thus, around 7.3 per cent of the total capital invested in all industrial sectors up to the end of 2000 was in SMIs.

Private sector involvement in SMIs

Recognizing the entrepreneurial and employment potential of SMIs, Qatar has paid significant attention to the promotion of SMIs through private sector participation in overall industrial development. In order to encourage private sector investment in SMIs, an industrial estate for these industries was established in the early 1970s at Salwa on the outskirts of Doha. As Salwa Industrial Estate is now fully occupied, a new industrial estate with an area of 11 square kilometres is under construction and due to open by 2003.

The Department of Industrial Development (DID), Ministry of Energy and Industry is the focal point for SMI activities. The DID is involved in studies, as well as licensing and control, of SMIs. The DID is also involved in project evaluation and in offering advice to the private sector on project proposals submitted for obtaining industrial licences. The DID also coordinates with institutions related to industry such as Qatar Industrial Development Bank (QIDB) and Qatar Industrial Manufacturing Company (QIMCO).

Industrial incentives and promotional efforts

Pre-investment promotional efforts and incentives

The DID is involved in promotional activities and offers the following incentives and services to SMIs:

- It explores industrial investment opportunities, prepares project profiles of techno-economically sound project ideas based on local raw materials and holds symposia and seminars for the promotion of these projects periodically for the benefit of national and foreign investors.

- It evaluates techno-economic feasibility studies submitted to the department by the private sector and offers technical advice on them.

- It carries out surveys on locally available raw materials and minerals and evaluates their quality, quantities and industrial properties as well as the suitability of these materials for industrial projects.

- It surveys locations and areas suitable for industrial projects in the industrial estates and establishes new industrial estates.

- It assists project promoters in their applications for industrial loans from QIDB, commercial banks and other financial institutions, whether local or foreign.

- It offers to the prospective investors upon their request all data, information and studies available at the department at a nominal fee.

- It allocates developed land plots for industrial projects on long-term leases at token rental rates.

Fiscal incentives

The Qatari government offers the following fiscal incentives:

- Exemption from customs duties on machinery, equipment, spare parts, manufactured and semi-manufactured goods used in local industry and packing materials.

- Waiver of corporate tax for five years from commencement of production.

- Exemption of national products from export tax.

- Supply of power, fuels, water and natural gas at internationally competitive prices.

- Establishment and development of fully serviced industrial estates.

- Financing of SMIs through QIDB (see Chapter 5.4) at low interest rates and with suitable grace periods for repayment of principal amounts.

- Liberal immigration rules and regulations to enable employment of foreign industrial labour.

Relative advantages and disadvantages in investment in, SMIs

Advantages of investments in SMIs include:

- social and political stability;

- a free economy with no restrictions on exchange transactions and money transfers by way of repatriation of dividends and principal amounts invested;

- the whole of Qatar as a free trade economic zone;

- stable exchange rate of the Qatari riyal against the US dollar (US$1 = QR3.65);

- a low rate of inflation.

Disadvantages to investment in SMIs include:

- the small size of the local market necessitating export, particularly to other GCC (Gulf Cooperation Council) countries;

- non-availability of local labour or technical and managerial talent;

- non-availability of a broad range of minerals, industrial raw materials or agricultural products.

Industrial estates for SMIs

Salwa Industrial Area

Located on Salwa Road, 10 kilometres west of Doha, this 28-square kilometre area was developed specifically for light and medium-scale industries. It hosts industries such as those producing dairy products, soft drinks, ready-to-wear clothing, wood products, paints, detergents, plastics, bricks, tiles, marble, steel- and aluminium-based metal products, household utensils and air conditioning equipment. In addition, there are a number of engineering works and printing and publishing houses.

All essential services such as electricity, water and telecommunications were installed from the outset and a good road network provides easy access to and within the industrial area.

New small- and medium-scale industrial area in Doha

As the Salwa Industrial Estate is now fully occupied, the government is developing a new industrial estate for SMIs. An agreement with a consultancy firm was signed in August 1998 for the development of a new 11-square kilometre industrial area to the west of the Salwa Industrial Area specifically for further SMIs under the direct administration and control of the DID. Developed land plots and industrial units will be allotted to holders of industrial licences from 2003.

The new industrial area is being developed in stages. Each stage has three phases at an overall cost of QR500 million (US$137.4 million). The DID has completed the basic studies, plans and engineering designs, and Stage 1 of the project, which covers around 40 per cent of the total surface of the industrial area, is expected to be completed by mid-2002.

From the above, it is clear that the government, through the Ministry of Energy and Industry, is keen to encourage the private sector through the provision of suitable facilities and incentives. Foreign participation in joint ventures through the supply of technology, equipment, marketing support and equity participation is encouraged. Although Qatar is a small market, foreign participants are encouraged by the relatively strong position of the country given its abundant energy resources, fiscal incentives, and friendly and congenial investment climate.

2.3

Foreign Investment Law

*David Silver, Solicitor, Hassan A AlKhater
Law Office, Doha, Qatar*

The investment of foreign capital in economic activity in Qatar is governed by the Foreign Investment Law, Law No. 13 of 2000. While reserving the fields of banking, insurance, commercial agency and dealing in real estate to Qatari nationals or entities wholly owned by one or more Qatari nationals, it creates the general rule that foreign investment in economic activity in Qatar must be made through a locally incorporated company that is at least 51 per cent owned by Qatari interests.

The Foreign Investment Law goes on to establish two exceptions to this general rule. The first is that, in the case of a foreign company which is awarded a contract in Qatar the performance of which is deemed by the Minister of Economy and Commerce to result in a service for the public benefit, the Minister may exempt such company from the general rule and permit the registration of an office of that company in Qatar without any local participation. However, such registration is strictly limited to the performance of the contract in respect of which it is given.

The second exception is that, in the case of a project in the field of agriculture, manufacturing, health, education, tourism, the development and use of natural resources or in the generation of power or mining and in the case of projects which have the objective of the transfer of an internationally recognized industry to Qatar or which promote national human resources, the Minister has a discretion to permit up to 100 per cent foreign ownership of the project capital. In making his decision, the Minister must have regard to whether the project is consistent with the State development plan and must give preference to projects that ensure the best use of locally available raw materials, projects which produce goods for export, projects which manufacture a new product or projects which use advanced technology. Although at least one such approval has already been given permitting 70 per cent foreign ownership of the capital of the company concerned, it is difficult to predict how discretion will be exercised by the Minister in practice as the executive regulations to be promulgated under the Foreign Investment Law have not yet been issued.

The Foreign Investment Law goes on to provide that land may be allocated to a particular project on the basis of a long-term lease not exceeding 50 years, with an option to renew. Further attractions provided for include the prospect of a tax holiday not exceeding a period of 10 years from the date of the commencement of operations. In addition, grants may be available to the project together with exemption from customs duties on the importation of machinery and equipment necessary for the construction of the project and on imports of raw and semi-finished materials required in the production process and which are not available in the local market.

Article 8 of the Law provides a guarantee against expropriation of the foreign investment except in circumstances where it is in the public interest to do so. In such circumstances, the Law provides that the expropriation will be done in an unbiased manner and on the basis that the foreign investor will be 'adequately' compensated. Adequate compensation is defined as being equal to the real economic value of the expropriated investment at the time of expropriation, or the announcement of it, based on a true economic value of the investment prior to any threat of expropriation. The compensation payable is to be paid without delay and is to be freely transferable. Interest is expressly stated to accrue on compensation until settlement at the then prevailing bank interest rate in Qatar.

The Foreign Investment Law also provides that the foreign investor will have the right to transfer freely, and without delay, any returns on the investment, the proceeds of any sale or liquidation of all or part of the project, any amounts received from the settlement of any dispute relating to the investment, or any compensation received in respect of any expropriation.

It is interesting to note that the Foreign Investment Law gives a statutory basis for the current practice of the Civil and Commercial Court in Qatar to recognize the rights of the parties to a contract to choose to resolve any dispute arising under that contract by way of local or international arbitration.

The Foreign Investment Law expressly provides that it does not apply to foreign companies that are extracting, exploiting or managing natural resources of Qatar through a concession agreement except to the extent that the application of the Law does not conflict with the terms of that concession agreement. The Law will also not be applicable to joint-stock companies formed between the government and one or more foreign investors pursuant to Article 90 of the Commercial Companies Law, Law No. 11 of 1981.

Part Three

Company Operational Issues

3.1

Forms of Intellectual Property

Sami Shafi Younis, Abu-Ghazaleh Intellectual Property, TMP Agents, Doha, Qatar

Trademarks

Trademark Law was effected in Qatar by Law No. 3 of 1978, by virtue of which trademarks are protected by being registered at the Trademark Office.

Qatar follows the international classification of goods and services. Service marks are protected according to the Trademark Law. A separate application should be filed with respect to each class of goods or services. Classes 1, 4–7, 10–14, 16–22, 29 and 31 are not entirely granted by the Trademark Law. Products covered by class 33 and 'alcoholic drinks and beverages' in class 32 are not registrable.

Once a trademark application is filed, it will be examined as to its form and substance, as Qatar follows the anteriority examination system. Trademark applications accepted by the registrar are published in the official gazette of trademarks. Any interested party may, within four months from the date of publication, oppose the registration of the trademark. The opposition case is referred to the Civil Court if not settled before the registrar, or if either party appeals against the registrar's decision. However, in the absence of opposition, a published trademark is registered and a relative registration certificate issued.

A trademark is valid for 10 years from the date of filing the application and may be renewed for further consecutive periods of 10 years. Renewal fees are paid during the last year of the current protection period with a six-month grace period, but such renewal is subject to payment of additional fees.

The ownership of a registered trademark cannot be assigned except with the enterprise (business) concerned. Unless an assignment has been recorded in the register and published in the official gazette of trademarks, the assignment will have no effect *vis-à-vis* third parties. Changes in the name and/or address of a registrant, amendment of a trademark not affecting substantially its identity, and limitation of goods or services covered by a registration can also be recorded.

The use of trademarks in Qatar is not compulsory for filing applications for registration or for maintaining trademark registrations in force. Any interested party may request the court to cancel the trademark from the register if, during five consecutive years from the date of registration, the owner has failed to use such trademark in Qatar.

Unauthorized use of a trademark registered under the Law or an imitation of such trademark applied on goods and/or services of the same class, or sale, storing for the purpose of sale, or exhibiting for sale of goods bearing a counterfeit mark, or using a mark duly registered under the Law by another person to serve the purpose of unauthorized promotion of goods and/or services of the same class are offences punishable under the Law.

Multi-class applications are not permitted by the Trademark Law. Each class of goods or services is considered to be an independent application.

According to Article 13 of the Trademark Law, the applicant for registration of a mark may enjoy the right of priority on the grounds of an earlier application filed in another country or state on the following conditions:

- The other state must be treating Qatar reciprocally.

- The applicant must append to his application a declaration indicating the date and number of the earlier application and the state in which it was filed.

- The applicant must file, within a period of six months after the date of submission of the earlier application, a copy of the earlier application certified as correct by the competent authority in the other state.

- Every detail of the application should be identical to the prior application.

Article 26 of the Trademark Law stipulates the following in respect to the recording of licences:

- The owner of a mark may, by contract, grant to any other natural person or legal entity a licence to use the mark for all or part of the goods or services in respect of which the mark is registered. The duration of the licence cannot be longer than the legal protection period of the mark.

- The licence agreement must be made in writing and must be signed by the contracting parties.

- The licence agreement must be recorded in the register on payment of the prescribed fee. Licensing will have no effect against third parties until it has been recorded in the register and published in the *Trademarks Bulletin*.

- The recording of a licence shall be removed from the register at the request of the owner of the mark or the licensee, after submission of evidence proving the termination or cancellation of the licence.

- In the absence of provision to the contrary in the licence agreement, the owner of the mark will have the right to grant licences for the use of the mark and continue to use it himself.

- In the absence of provision to the contrary in the licence agreement, a licence will not be assignable to third parties and the licensee will not be entitled to grant sub-licences.

According to the Trademark Law, the trademarks registrar is not allowed to record a change of name, address, merger, assignment, licence etc for pending applications. A recording of an assignment can only be effected for registered trademarks.

Assignment can be recorded with or without goodwill. A consideration should be stated in the deed of assignment. The amount can be any nominal figure – for example, US$1.

Documentation and other requirements

New trade-/service mark applications

For new applications, the following are required:

- a power of attorney signed by an authorized signatory and stamped with the company seal;

- a copy of a certificate of incorporation/good standing or an extract from the commercial register of the applicant company, duly legalized by a Qatari Consulate abroad;

- five copies of the trademark;

- a legalized home registration certificate is required only for claiming priority;

- specification of goods to be covered by the applications (classes are identical to international classification, including services);

- name, nationality, address, profession and legal status of the applicant.

Assignment applications

Assignment applications require:

- a power of attorney signed by an authorized signatory and stamped with the company seal by the assignee company;

- a deed of assignment signed by both parties, authenticated and legalized by the Qatari Consulate (if any), or any Arab Consulate available in the mark holder's country;

- a legalized certificate of incorporation/good standing or extract from the commercial register of the assignee company.

Registered user/licence agreement applications

Registered user/licence agreement applications require:

- an authenticated licence agreement in writing signed by the parties thereto and legalized by the Qatari Consulate in the country of origin;

- a power of attorney signed by an authorized signatory and stamped with the company seal by the licensee company;

- a legalized certificate of incorporation/good standing or extract from the commercial register of the registered user company.

Change of name/address applications

Change of name/address applications require:

- a power of attorney signed by an authorized signatory and stamped with the company seal in the new name and address;

- a certificate proving the change of name or address duly legal-ized by the Qatari Consulate (if any), or any Arab Consulate available in the country of origin.

Trademark alteration applications

Trademark alteration applications require:

- a power of attorney signed by an authorized signatory and stamped with the company seal;

- an authenticated certificate showing the amendment and duly legalized by the Qatari Consulate (if any), or any Arab Consulate available in the country of origin.

The recording of a merger

The following are required for the recording of a merger:

- a power of attorney signed by an authorized signatory and stamped with the company seal by the surviving company;

- an authorized certificate showing the merger and duly legal-ized by a Qatari Consulate abroad, or in its absence, any Arab Consulate.

Patents

There is no statutory Patent Law in force in Qatar; therefore, the only available means of protecting patents is by publishing cautionary notices in Arabic and English in appropriate period-icals. Cautionary notices define the owner's interest in the industrial property and announce the ownership thereto, and also alert the public against any possible infringement. Such public-ation of notices could be of considerable assistance in the case of litigation.

GCC patents

It is now the case that the GCC Patent Law is effective through filing at the Patent Office in Riyadh, Saudi Arabia, which began accepting applications on 3 October 1998. This application provides protection for all GCC member states – namely, Bahrain, Kuwait, Oman, Qatar, Saudi Arabia and the United Arab Emirates.

Designs (industrial models)

There is no statutory Design Law in force in Qatar; therefore, the only available means of protecting designs is by publishing cautionary notices in Arabic and English in appropriate periodicals.

Copyright

The Copyright Law, Law No. 25 of 1995 was issued on 22 July 1995. Protection is granted to authors of literary, artistic and scientific works whatever the value, kind or purpose of the writing or their means of expression. In general, the protection is provided for the works whose means of expression is writing, sound, drawing, image or motion picture. It also includes creative titles and computer software.

The right to protection belongs to those who, with permission from the original author, translate the work into another language, or those who summarize or modify the work, explain or comment on it to produce a new form of the work, without prejudice to the rights of the original authors.

The protection also covers the right of the author and the right of whoever translates a work into a foreign language, in translating that work into Arabic if the author or translator did not claim this right by himself or through others after three years from the date of publishing the original or translated work.

Protection is applicable to nationals whose works are published inside and outside the country and the works of non-nationals that are published in Qatar for the first time, as well as the works of authors of any other foreign country that deals with Qatari authors' works on a reciprocal basis.

The Copyright Law sets three conditions for licensing the publishing, display or circulation of a literary work:

1. The work must be accompanied by a certificate of origin showing the author's name or the name of the person who surrenders the right of usage.

2. The work must be accompanied by a permit from the supplier or owner for display or circulation, showing the geographic areas where the display and circulation is licensed.

3. The work must be accompanied by a supplier's certificate showing that publication rights are met whether through paying

the charges of putting the work to use by the public, or by making copies of the work for distribution.

In its third chapter, the Copyright Law deals with the rights of the author. It stipulates for the author:

1. The right to attribute to himself his work and to put his name on all the copies produced from it whenever the work is put to public use, except when the work is mentioned accidentally in a radio or TV presentation of current events. This right is inalienable and is not abolished with the passage of time.

2. The right to decide the publishing of his work, recording or displaying it and determining the entailed conditions and terms.

3. The right to use his work, on condition that he does not surrender that right to another person. However, it is inadmissible to use any work through transferring it to the public in Qatar except by a written, authenticated admission from the author or from his representative or his successor in the event of his death.

According to the Copyright Law, only the author is allowed to modify his work or translate it into another language during his lifetime. Heirs to the author can exercise the right of translation after the author's death. Only the author has the right to publish his letters and has the right of transfer of the financial rights that his work entails, according to the provisions of the Law, to one person or to multiple persons.

The author has the right to defend against any violation of his rights and has the right to prevent any elimination, addition, change or deformation in his work.

The Copyright Law determines the legitimate uses of protected works, even if they are not accompanied by the agreement of the author. It also sets other cases for the freedom of usage of protected works.

It is admissible, without the permission of the author, to copy news, political, economic, social, cultural or religious articles published in newspapers or periodicals, and other radio works of similar nature, on condition that the source and name of the author is mentioned clearly.

The fifth chapter of the Copyright Law provides rules for the work after the death of the author. It explains that the rights of the author provided in the Law are all or partly alienable whether through inheritance or legal process.

In its sixth chapter, the Copyright Law focuses on joint participation in the work. It states that if more than one person is involved in writing the work, where it becomes impossible to determine the separate share of each one in the joint work all participants will be considered equal partners in the ownership of the work, unless they agree otherwise.

No partner can individually exercise the copyrights except through the agreement of all the partners in writing. If a dispute arises among them, the dispute should be referred to the legal process.

All participants in the work have the right to file a legal case if the copyrights are violated. The copyrights transfer to the heirs of any of the participants.

If more than one person contributed to the writing of one work, where each one's role could be separated then each one will have the right to use his own part individually on condition this does not prejudice the right to use the joint works, unless they agreed otherwise. In its ninth chapter, the Copyright Law sets penalties for the violation of its provisions.

Applications for the registration of copyrights are deposited with the bureau in charge of protecting copyrights, the Copyright Protection Office. The implementing regulations of the Law have not yet been issued.

The future

At the WIPO Seminar held in November 2000 in Doha, it was declared that Qatar would implement a Statutory Industrial Design Law, Geographical Indications Law and Tradename Law 'shortly'. These have yet to be introduced however.

3.2

Privatization

Finbarr Sexton, Ernst & Young,
Doha, Qatar

Since independence, the Qatari government has, of necessity, maintained control of certain key economic sectors including oil and gas production and refining, the petrochemical industry and telecommunications. However, in recent years the government has adopted a clear policy of transferring ownership and responsibility for the development of specific business sectors to private investors.

Government objectives

Wider share ownership

There is a clear intent to distribute the ownership of wealth more widely in the economy, giving citizens a direct stake in the successful growth in the industrial and service sectors.

Greater efficiency

Privatized businesses are more likely to be responsive to customer-changing demand patterns; to exhibit a more flexible approach to decision making, and to more readily embrace a culture of profit optimization and cost reduction.

Best value for each sector sold

The government has relied heavily on foreign borrowings to develop the infrastructure for the Ras Laffan gas-based industrial sectors; it has been keen to arrive at a sale value that is both fair to the private investor and also maximizes government returns for reinvestment in other essential business sectors.

Strategies

The government has adopted a number of differing strategies in recent years to promote privatization.

Corporatization

Government organizations are reorganized along business lines, with a board of directors responsible for business decisions and a mandate to operate according to commercial principles. Examples of these initiatives included the corporatization of the Customs and Ports Authority, Civil Aviation Authority and postal services in 2001. These initiatives should assist these organizations in adopting more flexible decision-making processes, enhancing their customer focus and positioning the entities for the possible introduction of private investors at a future date.

Management contracts/outsourcing

The operation of a government-owned facility or service is contracted out to a private company. The government is currently assessing a number of such initiatives including appointing private firms to manage and develop abattoirs, parks and recreational areas, and the implementation of a city-wide parking meter system.

Divestiture/initial public offering (IPO)

The government has adopted a policy of privatization by initial public offering (IPO) of shares for larger government organizations. This strategy has been utilized where there is a clear institutional/public demand for the share offering and the proceeds of the share offering justify the cost of proceeding with the issue.

In December 1998, the government completed an IPO of 45 per cent of the shares of the state-owned Qatar Telecommunications Corporation. In March 1999, the government began the restructuring of the Ministry of Electricity and Water (MEW) with the ultimate objective of privatizing the electricity and water services sector. In May 2000, the assets owned by the MEW were transferred to a new company, Qatar General Electricity and Water Corporation (QGEWC). The company is 57 per cent owned by local investors and 43 per cent government owned.

In February 2002, the government approved an IPO for 55 per cent of the shares in Qatar Fuel Company, a newly established company to take over the distribution of petroleum products in the local market.

Private infrastructure development and operation

A private infrastructure development and operation strategy entails the private sectors building, financing and operating public infrastructure projects recovering costs through user charges. In 2000, the government transferred a number of functions at Doha International Airport to Qatar Airways Company. These functions included baggage-handling facilities and the development and operation of duty-free facilities at the Doha terminal.

In October 2001, the first greenfield independent power and water project was approved with the establishment of Ras Laffan Power Company.

It is expected that further private infrastructure development projects will be approved in coming years and a number of international investors are already seeking opportunities to develop infrastructural projects on a build-operate-transfer (BOT) and build-own-operate-transfer (BOOT) basis.

Joint ventures

The downstream oil and gas industry has been developed on the basis of joint venture companies comprising an international oil company with proven credentials in a specific downstream sector and the government, represented by Qatar Petroleum (QP). In such a joint venture, public and private resources and experience are pooled and the roles and responsibilities are arranged so as to facilitate the successful development of the project and ensure the transfer of technology and know-how to QP.

Such joint ventures have proved to be very successful and rewarding for the partners in the petrochemical, steel, fertilizer and liquefied natural gas (LNG) sectors.

A number of other sectors are targeted for privatization, including the hotel and steel industries. The Ministry of Finance has also initiated a study on how to offer a share in existing companies in the downstream oil and gas sector to local private investors. The government has also introduced incentives for private investment in the health sector in order to facilitate the improvement in overall medical services in the country and to reduce undue reliance on the state-administered clinics and general hospital network.

Incentives to attract further private sector investment

The government has been very successful in attracting international private sector investment in large-scale oil and gas projects. The development of the small-to-medium-scale industrial sector has been problematic however and remains a key government objective for future years.

Relaxation of restrictions on foreign inward investment

On 16 October 2000, the government enacted the Foreign Capital Investment Law, Law No. 13 of 2000, which is aimed at promoting further private sector investments into Qatar. The key provisions of the Law are summarized below.

Investment in land

Foreigners are not entitled to own land in Qatar. However, land may be allotted to projects established by foreign investors under long-term rental contracts for periods of up to 50 years, and to include renewable options thereafter.

Commercial, industrial, agricultural and service activities

The Law sets out the general principle that foreign participation in business activities in Qatar is allowed in all sectors of the national economy with the exception of the banking, insurance, commercial agency and real estate trading sectors. In general, the percentage of foreign ownership in business activities in Qatar should not exceed 49 per cent of the capital.

However, the percentage of foreign ownership may be increased to 100 per cent in the following designated business sectors:

- agriculture;
- manufacturing;
- health;
- education;
- tourism;
- projects which develop and utilize natural resources;
- power;
- mining.

A resolution from the Minister of Economy and Commerce is required in order to increase the foreign investment share above the general limit of 49 per cent. The Minister will consider the following factors in determining whether to approve the majority foreign participation in a business:

- the business project should be consistent with the development plans of the State;
- preference will be given to projects which:
  - use locally available raw materials;
  - manufacture products for export;
  - produce a new product or use advanced technologies;
  - facilitate the transfer of technology and know-how to Qatar;
  - promote the development of national human resources.

Contracting

The Minister may provide commercial licences to international contracting companies to register business entities in Qatar in the case where the international contractor is involved in the performance of a service for the public benefit.

Banking and insurance

The banking and insurance sectors are reserved for Qatari-owned entities. Foreign banks and insurance companies are allowed to operate under special foreign branch licences. However, the number of foreign branches operating in Qatar is restricted. The approval for the introduction of a new international bank into the Qatari market requires a recommendation to the Council of Ministers from the Qatar Central Bank (QCB) that an additional foreign branch of an international bank is desirable. Similar considerations apply to the introduction of a new foreign insurer into the Qatari market.

Part Four

The Fiscal and Regulatory Framework

4.1

Accounting Principles and Reporting Requirements

Finbarr Sexton, Ernst & Young, Doha, Qatar

Introduction

Qatar is anxious to attract inward investment from foreign companies for major industrial projects in the country. The Qatari government is also conscious of the need for foreign investors to have confidence in its financial and regulatory reporting regimes.

In the absence of national accounting principles and practices, the Ministry of Economy and Commerce has accepted the adoption of standards promulgated by the International Accounting Standards Board (IASB) as national accounting standards. In 1995, the Ministry of Economy and Commerce issued instructions to all public companies that annual financial statements should be drawn up in accordance with International Accounting Standards (IAS). A separate set of accounting standards and principles for banks was also approved by the Qatar Central Bank (QCB) in 1996. The standards issued by the QCB are similar to the pronouncements of the IASB.

Stock market influences on financial reporting

The Doha Securities Market (DSM) commenced operations in May 1997, listing the shares of Qatari public shareholding companies. At the end of 2001, there were 21 companies listed on the exchange. DSM management has encouraged the need for increased transparency by requiring the financial statements of quoted companies to become more widely available. It has also established clear guidelines for financial reporting by new entrants to the market and has taken an active role in promoting improved standards of reporting by the companies already listed on the DSM.

Statutory requirements

All business enterprises are required to maintain adequate financial records. These need not be maintained in Arabic however. The accounting and reporting requirements for companies with limited liability (WLL) are established in the Commercial Companies Law, Law No. 11 of 1981. Income tax regulations specify that taxable income must be recorded in accordance with the accruals basis of accounting. They also specify that all original documents must be available for inspection and that the books and records must consist of a general ledger, inventory books and subsidiary ledgers appropriate to the business activity. The financial year for a company is the Gregorian year unless the company's articles of association provide otherwise.

Financial reporting requirements

Filing requirements

For public shareholding companies, the audited balance sheet, income statement, directors' report and auditors' report must be submitted to the Ministry of Economy and Commerce within six months of the company's financial year end. A representative of the Ministry of Economy and Commerce is required to be present at the general assembly of shareholders.

Similarly, audited financial statements of limited liability companies whose capital exceeds QR500,000 must be submitted to the Ministry of Economy and Commerce within 10 days of the general assembly meeting. All companies with limited liability are obliged to hold a general meeting at least once a year.

Income tax regulations specify specific reporting requirements for taxpayers. In addition to the generally accepted reporting requirements, taxpayers are required to support audited financial statements with detailed analyses of fixed assets and depreciation calculations.

Interim financial reporting

All companies listed on the DSM are required to prepare half-yearly interim financial statements. Although there is no formal requirement to have these statements reviewed by independent accountants, most companies listed on the market have opted to have a review report issued on the interim accounts for shareholder protection.

The interim financial statements must meet the requirements of IAS 34, *Interim Financial Statements*.

Disclosure requirements

The QCB regulates the financial reporting and disclosure requirements for commercial banks, exchange houses, finance companies and investment companies operating in Qatar. These entities are required to furnish the QCB with monthly accounts in a specified format and to prepare comprehensive financial statements on an annual basis based on the QCB banking standards applicable to commercial banks and IAS for other financial services entities. The Ministry of Economy and Commerce has recommended the adoption of the standards promulgated by the IASB for other commercial entities operating in Qatar.

Audit requirements

All limited liability companies whose capital exceeds QR500,000 and all public shareholding companies should have auditors appointed by the general assembly every year. In addition, all final income tax declarations must be accompanied by financial statements audited by an auditor registered and based in Qatar.

The auditor must be independent of the company being audited and must be registered in the Register of Auditors as provided by Law No. 7 of 1974 – Organization of the Auditing Profession, which regulates the auditing profession.

Auditors' responsibilities

A company's auditors must report on every set of accounts laid before the company in general assembly. In their report, the auditors have to express their opinion on whether the balance sheet and profit and loss account present a fair view of the financial position, that they are in agreement with the actual state of affairs of the company and whether they contain all that is required by law and the company's articles of association. An auditor must also report whether the stocktaking procedure has been conducted according to established principles, whether regular accounts have been kept by the company, whether the auditor has obtained all the information which is considered necessary for the satisfactory performance of the auditor's duties, whether the information contained in the report of the board of directors is in agreement with the accounting records of the company and whether any violations of the provisions of law or of the articles have occurred during the financial year in a manner as to influence the activity or financial standing of the company.

Accounting profession

There is no accounting body in Qatar that has primary responsibility for issuing pronouncements on professional ethics, by-laws and accounting and auditing standards. However, the Ministry of Economy and Commerce regulates the activities of audit firms in Qatar and maintains the Register of Auditors.

Taxation of Business Activities

Finbarr Sexton, Ernst & Young, Doha, Qatar

Underlying principles

Law No. 11 of 1993 – Income Tax Regulations – was issued on 14 July 1993 to cover the income tax system and filing procedure in Qatar. The Law is supported by a set of tax practice directives enacted in Decision No. 3 of 1995 issued on 1 April 1995. In general, the Law provides that any business activity carried out in Qatar will be subject to tax. An 'activity' here is defined as any occupation, profession, service, trade or the execution of a contract or any other business for the purpose of making profit. Income tax is levied on foreign individuals, partnerships and companies operating in Qatar whether they operate through branches or in partnership with foreign companies.

Tax is not levied on Qatari-owned businesses. Law No. 9 of 1989 – Regulating granting parity to citizens of the Gulf Co-operation Council in taxation dealings – provides that, from 1 March 1989, nationals of Gulf Cooperation Council (GCC) countries are to be treated as Qatari citizens for income tax purposes. Accordingly, foreign companies wholly owned by Gulf nationals are not subject to income tax in Qatar.

Scope

Taxation is assessed on the basis of profits arising from activities in Qatar. Business profits include:

- profits on contracts executed in Qatar;
- profits on the sale of any of the company's assets;

- commission on agencies, representation agreements or commercial agencies whether the commission is realized in or outside Qatar;

- fees from consultancy, arbitration or expertise and other related services;

- rent from property;

- the sale, rent or assignment of concessions, trademarks, designs, know-how or copyrights;

- amounts received from debts previously written off;

- profits realized on liquidation;

- interest and other income from banks realized outside Qatar, which is subject to tax if it relates to amounts arising from a taxpayers activities in Qatar.

Taxable persons

Foreign entities carrying on business activities in Qatar are assessed for tax. The 1993 Income Tax Law specifically exempts the profits of wholly-owned Qatari companies from taxation. The Law also exempts the share of profits of Qatari individuals in business entities operating in Qatar.

Rates of taxation

The rates of taxation are shown in Table 4.2.1. The rates are applied on a progressive basis to the bands of income.

Table 4.2.1 Taxable income in Qatari riyals

Exceeding	Not exceeding	Rate (%)
0	100,000	Exempt
100,001	500,000	10
500,001	1,000,000	15
1,000,001	1,500,000	20
1,500,001	2,500,000	25
2,500,001	5,000,000	30
5,000,000		35

Tax administration and assessment

Tax accounting period

The Gregorian calendar year is to be used for Qatar income tax purposes. However, by way of exception a taxpayer may request in writing to prepare and submit tax filings for a year end other than 31 December. On commencement of activities, the first accounting period may be more or less than 12 months, but it should not be less than six months or more than 18 months.

When a taxpayer's activity is temporary or is for less than a six-month period, the taxpayer should submit a declaration when the activity is complete.

Filing and tax payment deadlines

Tax declarations should be filed within four months of the end of the financial period. Tax shown in the declaration becomes payable on the date at which the declaration becomes due for filing with the authorities.

Penalties

Penalties for late filing or late payment of taxes will be levied at the rate of QR10,000 per month or 2 per cent of tax due, whichever is greater. An additional penalty equal to 25 per cent of the tax liability arising on the undeclared income will be levied when the taxpayer:

- fails to declare all taxable income sources;

- does not declare all business activities;

- does not provide full information relating to the tax commitments of the business.

Tax submissions

Audited financial statements must support tax declarations where capital or annual profits of the business entity exceeds QR100,000. An accountant in practice in Qatar who is registered with the Ministry of Economy and Commerce must certify the financial statements. The tax authorities reject accounts certified by an auditor not resident and registered in Qatar.

Appeals procedures

The 1993 Income Tax Law establishes a formal tax appeals procedure against tax assessments issued by the tax department.

If the taxpayer does not agree with an assessment raised by the tax authority, he is required to lodge an objection letter within 30 days from the date of assessment. If the period expires without an objection, the assessment becomes final and cannot subsequently be appealed. However, if the taxpayer is still not satisfied with the authority's decision after the objection letter is lodged, he can appeal to a Tax Appeal Committee within 30 days of the date at which he is notified of the authorities' final decision. In addition, an appeal may also be presented to the High Court and finally to the Court of Appeal by either the taxpayer or the tax authority.

Computation of taxes

Incidence of taxation

Income tax is assessed on profits from income arising or deemed to arise from an activity in Qatar. Income is deemed to arise in Qatar when either of the following is located within the State:

- place of work or service performed;
- place of delivery of the work done;
- place of permanent office of the business.

At times it is difficult to make this distinction. The underlying premise is that income and profits arising must be deemed to have arisen in Qatar if the profits from the income relate to a contractual agreement negotiated in Qatar. However, this definition does not sufficiently clarify when and under what circumstances income is deemed to arise in Qatar. Many current business transactions demonstrate this point. For example, under current Qatari tax practice directives, a straight supply operation, FOB or CIF port of entry (or delivery to site by independent transporter), is not subject to Qatari tax. Such an operation is considered trade *with* Qatar, not trade *in* Qatar.

A taxpayer engaged in supply and installation contracts cannot claim exemption from reporting and accounting for the supply portion of the contract or project. Accordingly, all taxpayers engaged in supply and installation activities in Qatar will be required to report the gross value of revenues derived from such activities in their tax returns. The authorities permit a deduction for the supply value in accordance with an arm's length price (equivalent to international market value) for the supply operation.

Calculation of taxes

Taxable profits are calculated on the basis of profit disclosed by audited financial statements, adjusted for tax depreciation and any item disallowed for income tax purposes. The recognition of income and expenses should be determined by the accruals basis of accounting.

Deductions

Taxable income is ascertained after deduction of all costs and expenses incurred to earn that income. These include:

- interest expenses;

- rent paid;

- salaries and labour costs, end-of-service benefits and all related costs including charges allocated to end-of-service benefits, pension funds and other similar charges;

- fees and taxes other than income tax;

- debts written off that are approved by the tax authorities and which are in accordance with standards established for this purpose;

- gifts, donations, advertising and subscriptions for charitable, human, scientific, educational and sporting activities paid to government departments or other recognized associations or corporations in Qatar. The allowable cost is subject to a limit of 5 per cent of net profits before deduction of the cost.

The following costs and expenses are not considered tax-allowable items under the new tax regulations:

- personal and other expenses not related to taxable activities;

- criminal and tax penalties paid in accordance with the Tax Law;

- expenses or losses that may be recovered under an insurance policy or a contract, or by way of a compensation claim;

- depreciation of land;

- depreciation that exceeds cost;

- the branch share of head office expenses that exceed the rate determined by the tax authorities of total branch income.

The following additional issues are also of importance.

Head office expenses
The tax authorities have established specific thresholds on the permissibility of head office expenses. The present threshold is set at 3 per cent of turnover less subcontract costs. In the case of banks and insurance companies, the limit is 1 per cent.

The allowable ceiling for head office charges on a project that has income streams arising in Qatar and overseas is set at 3 per cent of total income after deducting subcontract costs, the supply value of imported machinery and equipment, revenues arising from work performed overseas, and other income which does not relate to activities in Qatar.

Depreciation
Depreciation of assets is allowable for tax in accordance with specific rates that are applied to cost on a straight-line basis. The rates applicable to the major asset categories are shown in Table 4.2.2

Table 4.2.2 Depreciation rates applicable to major asset categories

Asset category	Rate (%)
Buildings	4.0
Office furniture and equipment	15.0
Plant, machinery and equipment	15.0
Motor vehicles	25.0
Marine craft	7.5
Aircraft	25.0
Electrical equipment	20.0
Computers	33.33

If rates used in the financial statements are greater, the excess is disallowed. If lower rates are used in the financial statements, an additional claim is not permitted.

Provisions
General provisions such as bad debts and stock obsolescence are disallowed. Specific bad debts written off will be deductible to the extent that they are in accordance with the conditions set by the tax authorities.

Loss relief

The Tax Law contains provisions which allow for the carry forward of trading losses for set-off against future profits. Losses may be carried forward for a period not exceeding three years from the end of the tax year in which the losses were incurred. Losses cannot be set off against prior year income.

Powers of revenue assessment and tax collection

The tax authorities have the following powers of assessment and tax collection:

Deemed profit tax assessment

The Tax Law allows the tax authorities to issue an assessment for tax on a deemed profit basis in the following instances:

- if they have reasons to believe that the declaration submitted by the taxpayer is not correct;
- if the taxpayer fails to submit a declaration;
- if the taxpayer does not maintain proper books and records;
- if the taxpayer does not provide the information requested by the tax authority.

Collection of unpaid taxes from third parties

The Tax Law enables the tax authorities to request a statement from a third party of amounts owed to a taxpayer. The Law gives the tax authorities the power to collect these amounts directly from the third party.

Power to impound property of a taxpayer

The tax authority is empowered to seek a Ministerial Order that would enable it to impound a taxpayer's property for settlement of unpaid taxes.

Subcontractor payment withholding requirements

A practice directive issued by the Director of Income Tax in January 1993 requires all ministries, government departments, public and semi-public establishments and other taxpayers to withhold final payments to subcontractors until such entities present a tax clearance certificate issued by the Income Tax Department. The directive also imposes annual disclosure and compliance requirements on the principal contractor. The principal contractor must submit a listing of subcontractors to the Department, giving names, addresses, the value of each subcontract and variations in contract terms.

The tax clearance certificate furnished by the subcontractor must be submitted as a support for the final tax declaration of the principal contractor.

Tax exemptions

The Tax Law includes provisions for the award of tax exemptions for major projects executed by foreign or Qatari companies. The main conditions necessary for the successful award of a tax exemption are:

- that the projects contribute to the support of industry, agriculture, trade, oil, minerals, tourism, communications, or land reform, or any other activities or contracts that the country needs and which are of benefit both economically and socially;

- that the project falls within the planned development and economic objectives of the State and has the approval of the government department concerned;

- that the project contributes towards the national economy. The following points are considered:

  - the commercial profitability of the project;

  - the extent to which the project complements other projects;

- the extent to which the project utilizes material produced locally;

- the effect of the project on the balance of trade payments;

- that the project uses modern technology;

- that the project creates employment opportunities for citizens.

Any contractor involved in the execution of an exempt project can apply for exemption from income tax.

The tax exemption provisions are aimed at promoting foreign inward investment into Qatar.

Statutory limitation periods

Under the Tax Law, the government forfeits its right to claim taxes from taxpayers after the lapse of a five-year limitation period. However, the limitation period is revoked from the date at which the tax authorities notify the taxpayer to settle taxes due. A taxpayer forfeits his right to claim taxes overpaid after a three-year limitation period from the date of assessment.

General provisions

The provisions of the Tax Law do not apply to the following:

- salaries, wages, allowances and related items;

- interest and bank income due to natural persons;

- corporate societies;

- religious, charitable, cultural, educational and sports institutions licensed in Qatar;

- natural persons' profits resulting from the purchase and sale of land, real estate, shares or bonds;

- interest on public treasury bonds, development bonds and bonds of public corporations;

- agricultural activity and fishing;

- inheritance and legacies;

- profits of Qatari natural persons;

- shares of Qatari citizens in the profits of juristic persons.

Avoidance of double taxation

Qatar has two double tax treaties that are currently effective for tax planning: France and India. Tax treaties with a range of other countries are being reviewed including Belgium, Egypt, Russia and the United Kingdom.

Several countries, including Japan, the United States and the United Kingdom, allow some unilateral relief against their own taxes for Qatar income tax paid.

Taxation of individuals

The Tax Law does not extend to the taxation of the personal income of individuals. There are no personal taxes, social insurance or other statutory deductions from salaries and wages in Qatar. In addition, there are no estate or gift taxes applicable in Qatar. Income from private professions such as legal practices, consultancy services, and other sole trader activities are subject to income tax under guidance issued in Decision No. 3 of 1995.

Military contracts

In recent years, contracts awarded to foreign military equipment suppliers and contractors have enjoyed a special tax-exempt status. This status has been granted at the request of the Ministry of Defence and the Ministry of the Interior to ensure the confidentiality of the contracts.

Other taxes

Customs duties

Material and equipment for permanent use
The import of goods into Qatar is regulated by the Qatar Customs Law, Law No. 5 of 1988. The following rates of customs duty apply on goods imported into Qatar.

- General items   4%
- Cement   20%
- Steel   20%
- Tobacco   100%

The basic value for the assessment of duty is the CIF value of the goods. Where only the FOB price can be established, duty is based upon the FOB price plus 15 per cent.

Exemption from customs duty may be approved at the negotiation stage of commercial bids for projects.

Temporary imports

Under the current customs duty regulations, a contractor is allowed a temporary import exemption on major equipment. Temporary imports are subject to the prior approval of the Customs and Port Authority. This approval is normally valid for a period of six months, but may be extended by a further six months. After this period, the four per cent duty must be paid.

Legalization fees

Legalization fees represent an indirect 'tax'. Import documentation for shipments of goods and materials to Qatar must be legalized by the Qatari Embassy in the country of origin. Where no embassy exists, the legalization process may take place at the Ministry of Foreign Affairs in Qatar. The supplier is responsible for the legalization fees.

Legalization fees are levied on the CIF invoice value as follows:

Commercial invoice value (QR)			Fees (QR)
1	to	5,000	100
5,000	to	15,000	200
15,000	to	50,000	500
50,000	to	100,000	700
100,000	to	150,000	1,200
150,000	to	250,000	1,800
250,000	to	500,000	2,200
500,000	to	1,000,000	3,000
1,000,000	to	–	0.4% of value

4.3

Legal Environment

David Silver, Solicitor, Hassan A AlKhater
Law Office, Doha, Qatar

Introduction

Qatar is an absolute monarchy organized in accordance with a
provisional constitution promulgated on 19 April 1972 as a sover-
eign Arab Islamic state ruled by an Emir, who is advised by an
appointed consultative assembly and who appoints the members
of the Council of Ministers, Qatar's principal law-making body.

The Council of Ministers is responsible for proposing draft laws
and decrees. The Council of Ministers submits draft legislation
to the Emir for promulgation. The general rule is that legislation
only comes into effect one month after its publication in the *Official
Gazette*, unless some other date for its effectiveness is stipulated
in the legislation itself.

The judicial system is divided into two main divisions: the Civil
Court and the Shari'a (Islamic) Court. By custom, the Shari'a Court
has limited itself to the adjudication of disputes between Muslims
in matters of personal status such as marriage, inheritance and
certain criminal acts, although it may include commercial matters
if the parties to the action are Muslims or have voluntarily
submitted to its jurisdiction and the relevant proceedings are
initiated in the Shari'a Court. In practice, the Shari'a is unlikely
to have any impact on commercial disputes, which are dealt with
by the Civil Court pursuant to Qatari civil law.

Qatar has a level of business law comparable with neighbouring countries. The areas of business law commonly of interest to
foreign companies considering doing business in Qatar or investing in a business enterprise in the State are as follows.

Civil Law

The Civil and Commercial Law of the State of Qatar is promulgated by Law No. 16 of 1971, commonly known as the Civil Code. The Civil Code provides that the sources of law in Qatar are, first, any applicable statutory provision and, in the absence of such provision, the Court will look next at any special custom of the trade or business concerned, then to any local custom or practice and, finally, to the principles of Shari'a law. In practice, however, in the absence of any applicable custom or practice, the courts will turn to consider the laws of other Arab states.

Commercial Law

The Commercial Law is largely set out in the Civil Code. This provides a reasonably comprehensive law of contract. The main requirements of a binding contract are a mutual intention to be bound and certainty of the parties to the contract. The objects of the contract must be lawful and not contrary to public policy or morality. However, the Civil Code expressly provides a presumption of legitimacy in respect of every contract. In practice, this means that the contract will be deemed to be lawful and not contrary to public policy or morality unless the contrary is proved. The Civil Code also offers the parties to an international contract the right to choose the law that will govern that contract. The courts will recognize agreement between the parties to such a contract to the jurisdiction in which any dispute arising out of it will be heard. The parties are also entitled expressly to waive their respective rights of recourse to the Civil Court and to agree in writing that any dispute arising out of that contract will be resolved by arbitration.

The Civil Code deals with the creation, transfer and discharge of contractual obligations, the assignment of contractual rights, the rules relating to specific types of contracts such as FOB and CIF contracts of sale and has comprehensive sections dealing with bills of exchange, promissory notes and cheques. It also recognizes the expiry of contractual rights by the passage of time, the standard time-bar period being 15 years unless a shorter time is specified in the Law.

Companies Law

The Companies Law is set out in the Commercial Companies Law – Law No. 11 of 1981. This recognizes five types of company, including companies with limited liability (WLL), joint-stock companies and joint ventures. Foreign investors are generally limited to participating in a limited liability company or joint venture.

The Companies Law provides that a limited liability company must be composed of not less than two partners and not more than thirty. The company must have a capital of not less than QR200,000 (US$54,795). It does not issue negotiable shares and its capital is divided into equal units of not less than QR1,000 (US$274) each. Such companies are expressly prohibited from carrying on the business of banking, insurance or the investing of money for third parties. Once the company has been incorporated, each such unit acquires a right to vote in general assembly, to receive a share of the profits of the company, if any, and a share in the surplus or deficit resulting from a liquidation of the company. Each unit is capable of being sold or being transferred by way of gift or, on the death of a partner who is a natural person, to his heirs.

The basic document for incorporation of the company is the constitutive contract (equivalent to the memorandum and articles of association). The constitutive contract must be in writing and signed by each of the parties to it. The Companies Law sets out the minimum requirements for the constitutive contract, which includes the name of the company and the address of the principal office, the names of the partners, their nationalities and places of residence, the commercial objects of the company, the amount of the capital of the company, the amount paid by each partner and whether that has been subscribed in cash or in kind, any limitation on the right to dispose of any interest in the company, the term for which the company is incorporated, the names of those individuals appointed as the manager of the company and the method of distribution of profits and losses.

The Companies Law provides that the company must be run by one or more managers appointed by the partners who will be deemed to have full authority to represent the company unless the constitutive contract stipulates otherwise. The appointed manager(s) are responsible directly to the general assembly of the company.

It is also open to the foreign investor to enter into a joint venture with an entity already registered to carry on that business in Qatar. Two particular disadvantages of such an arrangement are that the joint venture would be carried on entirely in the name of the registered entity and the assets of that joint venture would be, *prima facie*, the assets of the registered entity. However, the Law provides that it is unlawful for a foreign entity to carry on in joint venture with a Qatari entity any business that is reserved only for Qatari nationals.

Property Law

Except for very limited circumstances, largely relating to reciprocal arrangements for the purposes of diplomatic representation, non-Arab nationals are unable to own real estate within Qatar. Property is therefore rented. There is only light statutory control over the leasing of real estate with wide freedom of negotiation.

Intellectual Property Law

Trademarks and commercial indications are registrable under the Trademark Law, Law No. 3 of 1978, subject to the ability to show a sufficient prior right to the use of that mark or indication, although the process of registration is lengthy. The Law permits the Ministry of Economy and Commerce, or the owner of such registered trademarks or commercial indications, to initiate action against the unlawful use of such trademark or commercial indication. In the case of the Ministry, that action would be to report the matter to the police for investigation with a view to criminal proceedings being taken against such unlawful use. In the case of the registered owner, the action would be by way of civil proceedings.

The Copyright Law, Law No. 25 of 1995 permits the registration of copyright and the protection of existing copyright in respect of a wide range of original works which may be written, oral or visual in nature or any combination and includes original works of an electromagnetic nature including, for example, computer programs. The Law provides penalties for the copying and sale of existing original works without the approval of the owner of the copyright or the owner's authorized representative and for the mandatory confiscation of any such copies.

The concept of licensing the use of commercial marks and indications or other intellectual property by the registered owner is also recognized.

Maritime Law

Qatar boasts a comprehensive Maritime Law, Law No. 15 of 1980. This deals with many topics including rights over vessels, priority rights, mortgages, the right to arrest and the rights and obligations of the master and the crew. The Maritime Law contains comprehensive chapters dealing with the exploitation of vessels including chartering and the contract of carriage both of cargo and passengers. The provisions relating to contracts of carriage broadly follow the Hague-Visby Rules.[1] The Law also deals with towing and pilotage, accidents at sea, assistance and salvage, general average and contracts of marine insurance relating both to vessels and cargo.

In international contracts, the Qatari courts will recognize a provision choosing the applicable law that will govern the contract. However, all proceedings brought before the courts are conducted in Arabic and any documentary evidence to be submitted to the courts which is not prepared in Arabic must be translated. It is very important, therefore, that a careful translation is made as the courts will rely on the text of the Arabic translation. Alternatively, the courts may be expected to recognize, and enforce, a clear agreement to arbitrate. As the parties to such an agreement are free to determine the language and the location in which the arbitration will take place, foreign entities doing business in Qatar should seriously consider incorporating agreements to arbitrate, including the language to be used in such arbitration, wherever appropriate in its agreements in respect of Qatar.

---

[1] Because of the lack of uniformity in the laws of different countries relating to bills of lading, a set of rules, known as the Hague Rules, was produced by an international conference at the Hague in 1922. The Hague Rules were widely adopted into law by the countries signing the resulting protocol. However, over time the shortcoming in the Hague Rules became apparent and the rules were reviewed and amended by a further conference in Brussels in 1968. The amended rules are known as the Hague-Visby Rules.

Procedures for Handling Legal Disputes/ Arbitration

David Silver, Solicitor, Hassan A AlKhater Law Office, Doha, Qatar

Litigation in the Civil Court is conducted in Arabic and all documents to be produced in evidence in Civil Court proceedings must be translated into Arabic. Once the petition commencing the proceedings has been filed with the Court and the appropriate fees paid, the Court will draw up the summons to the defendant attaching a copy of the statement of claim and any supporting documents. That summons, which specifies the date of the first hearing, is then served upon the defendant by an official of the Court.

At the date of the first hearing, the proceedings will be adjourned either on the basis of an application from the plaintiff for time to submit supporting documentation or, alternatively, by the defendant for the purpose of preparing a reply. If the defendant fails to appear at the first hearing, the Civil Procedure Code, Law No. 13 of 1990 requires that the case be automatically adjourned for the defendant to be re-served. In the event that the defendant fails to attend at the second hearing, the Court is free to proceed in the absence of the defendant.

The claim does not progress to a formal trial but proceeds by way of a number of subsequent hearings and adjournments during which the parties will prepare and serve written memorandums by way of reply and answer and exchange documentary evidence (if any). During the course of these hearings, any witnesses who are required to give oral evidence would be called to give testimony and to be cross-examined on that evidence. However, in commercial matters, the courts will rely on documentary evidence in preference to oral evidence in the determination of the issues before them.

Once the Court is satisfied that all evidence to be adduced by the parties has been submitted and all arguments completed, the Court will adjourn the matter for judgment. The defendant is granted the right of final comment. The Court has the authority to, and frequently will, appoint an expert to review the evidence in a particular case and to advise the Court in respect of a specific aspect of the claim upon which the Court requires expert guidance.

Judgments at the Court of First Instance become effective immediately on pronouncement and may be appealed by either party to the Court of Appeal. The Court of Appeal has sole jurisdiction to hear appeals on points of law or fact and conducts appeals before it by way of a re-hearing of the case. The issuing of an appeal does not, by itself, stay the judgment appealed against. A judgment of the Court of First Instance remains enforceable unless and until stayed by the Court of Appeal. A stay of any judgment would normally only be granted upon terms guaranteeing the payment of the judgment if the appeal is dismissed. The judgment of the Court of Appeal is final and binding on the parties.

The Civil Courts represent a reasonable forum for the resolution of commercial disputes. The courts are provided with a comprehensive code of procedure under Law No. 13 of 1990. Defended commercial proceedings may be expected to take between one and three years to come to judgment at first instance.

The Qatari courts currently recognize, and may be expected to enforce, a clear written agreement between the parties to arbitrate any dispute between them. The parties may choose to adopt the arbitral rules of such bodies as, for example, the International Chamber of Commerce, UNCITRAL, the London Court of International Arbitration or the American Arbitration Association. Alternatively, the Civil Procedure Code provides its own reasonably comprehensive rules of arbitration. However, in the context of alternative dispute resolution, it is important to note that under the provisions of the Civil Procedure Code, arbitrators are not authorized to conciliate, or to pass arbitral awards as conciliating arbitrators, unless they are specifically named in the agreement upon which the arbitration is based.

The Civil Procedure Code sets out the rules that apply to the enforcement of foreign judgments in Qatar. The basis for such enforcement is reciprocity and, in order to enforce a qualifying foreign judgment, the party applying to do so will be required to prove to the Qatari court the rules and procedure used to enforce Qatari judgments in the jurisdiction in which the judgment to be enforced was obtained.

Part Five

The Financial Structure and Banking System

5.1

Banking: An Overview

Commercial Bank of Qatar, Doha, Qatar
(www.cbq.com.qa)

The banking sector in Qatar is supervised by the Qatar Central Bank (QCB), which was established in 1993 as the successor to the Qatar Monetary Agency. The QCB acts as the government's agent to control the country's monetary policy, to monitor the commercial banking system and to regulate interest rates on Qatari riyal funds, while allowing other banks to float interest rates within specified limits. The QCB administers the country's relations with international financial agencies, acts as a banker for the government and issues currency notes and coins.

The QCB has introduced major international standards applicable to banking supervision and regulation based on the Basle Accord. The minimum capital adequacy regulations applicable to Qatari banks has been raised to 10 per cent from the previous Basle standard minimum rate of 8 per cent. The QCB has also implemented an automated link with local banks (the QCB-Link) to enhance its ability to monitor banks in a timely and accurate manner.

As part of the government's measures to implement reform in the financial sector, the Law Regulating Public Debt – Law Number (1) of 1998 – was approved in March 1998. This Law allows the QCB to issue treasury bills and bonds with the intent of widening the scope of participants at a later date to include local non-bank and foreign investors. The introduction of treasury bills and bonds has facilitated the ability of the monetary authorities to implement the optimal desired monetary policy by more active interventionary actions to influence the level of money supply and interest rates.

In February 2000, the QCB removed its last curb on interest rates by ending the 6.5 per cent ceiling set on riyal deposits of

12 months' duration or less. The QCB removed ceilings on interest rates for deposits of over 15 months and 12 months in 1997 and 1998, respectively. Freeing interest rates would help to reinvigorate the country's fledging financial market and attract domestic funds currently held in foreign currencies. The determination of lending rates has been left to the market since 1995.

The banking sector is comprised of 15 banks, eight of which are Qatari owned, including five commercial and two Islamic banks as well as the specialized Qatar Industrial Development Bank (QIDB). In addition, two Arab and five foreign banks are represented in Qatar (see below). The Commercial Bank of Qatar is rated the best among local banks by the international rating agency, Moody's. The Islamic banking system finances many projects under Islamic Shari'a law, under which interest is forbidden, therefore conducting the financing of business transactions on a profit-, or loss-sharing basis.

Qatar has a well-structured network of bank branches (92 in total, dispersed throughout the country), which provides the full range of banking services comprising personal, corporate, treasury and investment banking services. Electronic banking was introduced in 2001 by the Commercial Bank of Qatar, the only bank to provide an Internet-based banking service.

Major banks in Qatar have their main branches on Grand Hamad Street, a main thoroughfare in Doha, and local branches spread around Doha and other major towns. ATM machines are available on main streets, in bank branches, at shopping complexes and on larger company premises. Most ATM machines accept international cards such as Diners Club, Visa, Plus, MasterCard, Cirrus, NAPS, JCB and American Express. There is a well-established point-of-sale network in Qatar, also accepting all major credit cards.

Commercial banks operating in Qatar as at January 2002
(Information provided by the Qatar Central Bank)

Qatari banks
Qatar National Bank SAQ
Doha Bank Ltd.
Commercial Bank of Qatar QSC
Al-Ahli Bank of Qatar QSC
Grindlays Qatar Bank
Qatar Industrial Development Bank (QIDB)

Islamic banks
Qatar International Islamic Bank
Qatar Islamic Bank SAQ

Foreign banks
Arab Bank PLC
Mashreq Bank PSC
BNP Paribas
HSBC
Standard Chartered Bank PLC
United Bank Limited
Bank Saderat Iran

5.2

Insurance: An Overview

Ian Sangster, Assistant General Manager,
Qatar Insurance Company, Doha, Qatar

The market

For a number of years, the Qatari insurance market was marked by periods of slow growth due to the lack of sustained infrastructural and industrial development. As a consequence, there was little innovation within the market as there was little or no need for it.

The major insurable risks were Qatar Petroleum (QP; formerly Qatar General Petroleum Corporation, QGPC) and a number of downstream industries located at Mesaieed industrial city to the south of the capital, Doha.

However, Qatar has within its territorial borders the single largest offshore non-associated gas field in the world. This field, referred to as 'North Dome' or 'North Field', was discovered in 1971.

It was not until 1994 that it was decided to proceed with the development of the North Field and the marketing of natural gas. This momentous and bold decision led to the construction and operation of two world-class liquefied natural gas (LNG) plants involving investments in excess of US$10 billion. The astounding success of these ventures has resulted in multi-billion dollar expansion plans being undertaken.

Concurrent with the development of the natural gas field there were a number of added value downstream ventures established that utilized Qatar's hydrocarbons as their feedstock. The establishment of a number of other ventures will ensure that the expansion of the industrial base continues well into the first decade of this century.

The foregoing developments have resulted in the emergence of a more sophisticated insurance industry which now has to deal with the complexities of the large onshore and offshore developmental projects, many of which are the subject of project finance.

It will therefore be noted that there is a very active energy insurance sector involving both operational and construction insurance packages.

There are five national insurers and four foreign insurance companies operating within Qatar. One of the national insurers is founded upon, and operates within, Islamic principles.

The insurance industry is regulated by Decree Law No. 1 of 1964, which deals with the supervision and control of insurance companies and agents. The main element of interest to companies entering Qatar is the requirement that all insurance covers must be purchased locally. Essentially, non-admitted policies are forbidden. In any event, contracts undertaken within Qatar almost exclusively require local covers to be purchased.

Corporate insurance

The corporate sector dominates the insurance industry, with the vast majority of premiums being generated from this class of insurance.

Prior to the rapid developments that have been taking place in the energy sector since about 1994, the major trading houses and local contracting companies provided the main base of premiums for the insurance industry. The energy sector was very important but consisted of only a handful of accounts. At this time, foreign oil companies had not entered Qatar and the LNG industry was just about to commence construction of a major plant at Ras Laffan, north of Doha.

International companies entering Qatar to undertake projects will find that the conditions of contract call for related insurance programmes to be insured within Qatar by one of five national insurers. The contract may specify that the insurance covers should be arranged by the contractor (contractor placed), or by the principal (principal placed).

In the case of the latter arrangement, the insurance covers will invariably be the subject of competitive tender with each insurer utilizing the services of an international insurance broker and the support of the global reinsurance market.

In terms of the contractor-placed route, it is up to the individual company to approach an insurer of their choice locally in order to obtain quotations and negotiate relevant terms. It is not uncommon in these circumstances for companies entering Qatar to seek to negotiate a deal with a national insurer, which involves their worldwide insurance consultant and/or insurer(s).

The classes of business that would normally fall within the scope of contracts entered into are:

● contractors' all risks;

● third-party liability;

● workmen's compensation;

● contractors' plant and equipment;

● marine cargo.

Service is of increasing importance to large international companies entering or already operating in Qatar, but with a judicious choice of local carrier they should be able to obtain a level of service comparable with that to which they are accustomed in their home countries.

It is worth noting that, although there is a Labour Law (Law No. 3 of 1962) in force that regulates the employment of labour and their rights, it is not compulsory to insure in respect of work-related accidents or deaths. An exception is where a company is required to do so by contract. Most prudent employers will in any case insure their employees and transfer the risk to an insurance company.

Under the Labour Law, there is a maximum payment in the event of the work-related death of an employee of approximately US\$33,000. In the event of permanent disability, there is a scale of charges within the Labour Law that designates the percentage applicable to the particular injury. It should be noted that the Labour Law is one of strict liability, in that the accident need only be proved for the employer to be liable. It is not necessary to prove negligence.

However, an employer may well incur a common law liability in the event of the work-related injury being caused by the negligence of the employer. Cases of this nature will be dealt with within the Islamic Shari'a legal system and while the employer's liability is in theory unlimited, in practice the awards are made on multiples of the maximum award made under the Labour Law in the case of an employee's death.

To cater for this exposure, an employer's liability extension may be included within the workmen's compensation cover. This will provide protection in respect of Shari'a law awards up to the limit insured. This limit is chosen by the insured but an amount of US$2 million has been the most common up until now. It should be noted, however, that Qatar is becoming more litigious and it may not be long before claimants come forward seeking amounts of compensation higher than has traditionally been awarded.

Car insurance falls both within the corporate and personal insurance arena but is included in this section in view of its importance to the corporate risk manager. Third-party liability (public liability) cover is compulsory for all vehicles within Qatar; it is impossible to register a vehicle without producing a certificate of insurance together with its registration documents.

With regard to marine cargo, fire etc and liability insurance, companies will find that policy wordings to which they are accustomed in their home country will generally be available, by negotiation, in Qatar.

Personal insurance

Personal insurance has not been actively developed in Qatar until recently. The lack of an insurance culture resulted in insurance companies responding to specific requests for cover, predominately from expatriates, on an *ad hoc* basis. The most requested covers were householder, personal accident and medical. None of these insurances was requested in sufficient numbers to justify insurance companies establishing personal insurance departments. However, the establishment of a greater industrial base in recent years, the increase in the number of expatriates used to purchasing insurance and the levying of charges by the government on expatriates for medical services, have been major factors in the dynamics creating a nascent market for personal lines. A few of the insurance companies have responded by designing and developing insurance products for the retail market.

Leading the product range are medical insurance policies, spearheaded in 1999 by the 'QatarCare' scheme, the only low-cost cover available to cater for medical costs incurred within Qatar. This innovative cover filled a void that could not be met economically by the well-known but expensive international medical expenses policies. There is a considerable market now available to insurance companies in this line of business as both nationals and expatriates opt for private protection schemes.

As mentioned above, third-party motor (car) insurance is compulsory within Qatar. The insurance cover provided is in accordance with legislative requirements and provides for unlimited liability in respect of personal injury/death and loss or damage to third-party property. Comprehensive covers are available to motorists but currently in excess of 60 per cent of the motoring public purchase only the compulsory third-party cover. New products, such as extended period agency repairs and replacement vehicles while a driver's vehicle is in the garage for repair, are now available. As the insurance awareness of the general public increases further, there will be a significant market for the personal lines created.

In general, insurance companies do not see motor insurance as a profitable line of business. Third-party premiums were fixed by the Ministry of the Interior some years ago and have never been increased. The total premiums generated are generally insufficient to fund the annual claims.

Banks have been quick to offer protection to the individual borrower and have moved aggressively into the personal loan sector. They offer life cover to clients to pay off loans in the unfortunate event of the borrower's untimely death. The local insurance market underwrites these life schemes. In an effort to provide a 'one-stop shop' financial service, banks are now seeking to offer a wide range of personal insurance. Again, the local insurance market underwrites these covers.

5.3

Regulation of Banking and Financial Services

David Silver, Solicitor, Hassan A AlKhater Law Office, Doha, Qatar

Banking practice is regulated by Decree Law No. 15 of 1993, which established the Qatar Central Bank (QCB). The QCB is empowered to direct the monetary policy and banking credit of the country, issue and manage the circulation of currency, supervise and control banks and other financial institutions, act as banker to the government and to all banks operating in the country and manage the reserve funds allocated to support the currency.

The Law provides that the carrying on of banking business is prohibited except with a licence for that purpose granted by the Council of Ministers upon the recommendation of the QCB. Banking business is defined as the acceptance of deposits for use in banking operations, such as discounting, purchase or sale of negotiable instruments, granting loans, trading in foreign exchange and precious metals and any other activities which are considered to be banking business by commercial law or custom.

The control of the QCB has been extended to cover the business of money exchange by Law No. 36 of 1995 (Regulating the Business of Money Exchange). Applications for a licence may only be made by Qatari nationals and must be submitted to the QCB. Licences are issued by the Board of the QCB on the recommendation of the Governor. In the case of a rejection, application for review may be made to the Board within 30 days from the date of receipt of notice of refusal. However, the decision of the Board on such a review is final. Licences are renewable annually.

The control of banking and financial services is conducted by the QCB through circulars that it issues from time to time. These circulars cover all aspects of financial regulation including, for example, setting parameters for the licensing of companies established for the purposes of financing or investment. These parameters include the minimum share capital of such companies and the level of qualifications and experience of their senior management.

In terms of banking, the QCB regulates all aspects of business including, for example, reporting obligations, banking operations including the clearing of cheques, liquidity ratios, capital adequacy, the granting of credit, the prevention of money laundering, the maintenance and protection of records, the opening of branches and business hours and holidays.

In terms of financial services, QCB circulars regulate the conduct of each locally licensed financial institution in its relationship with its customer, whether the institution offers its own products or acts as intermediary for a financial institution outside the jurisdiction. Regulation extends to cover the contract entered into between the financial institution and its customer and any prospectus published by a locally licensed institution. The regulations include a requirement that such a prospectus and the contract between the financial institution and its customer must be in Arabic. Although the document may also be printed in both Arabic and a second language, Arabic is the text of reference and, in the case of discrepancies between the two, the Arabic text will prevail.

There is currently no legislation permitting the establishment of investment funds within Qatar. However, it is a widely held view that legislation dealing with this aspect of financial services is being prepared.

5.4

Qatar Industrial Development Bank (QIDB)

Shaikh Hamad Nasser AlThani Ph.D., General Manager, Qatar Industrial Development Bank, Doha, Qatar

The Qatar Industrial Development Bank (QIDB) is owned by the Qatari government and has an authorized and fully paid-up capital of QR200 million (US$55 million). It is the only specialized financial institution in the country engaged in the identification, development, promotion and financing of industrial projects.

The QIDB's main activities include:

- providing long-term loans (and equity in certain cases) to industrial projects to acquire fixed assets and imports of raw material;

- undertaking studies, providing advisory services, promoting attractive projects based on sound technology and providing assistance during project implementation.

The QIDB strives to achieve its objectives in a number of ways that include extending and/or guaranteeing financial assistance, assisting in obtaining finance from other institutions, providing export and import credit facilities, identifying and developing sound project opportunities, providing consulting services and guiding and monitoring projects during and after implementation.

With the new investment policy, the private sector is set to play a leading role in the economic development process in the coming years through investment in a large number of small and medium-sized projects – in which the QIDB seeks to be integral. To this end, the QIDB has chalked out a strategy of promoting attractive joint venture projects based on sound technologies from the industrial nations (with the equity participation of a technology holder); it prepares an investment study on behalf of the promoters and provides every support at all stages of project development.

The rate of interest charged by the QIDB for any loan is 50 per cent of the local commercial borrowing rate. Its financial assistance covers up to 80 per cent of the value of capital equipment, subject to a cap of 60 per cent of the total project cost or 10 per cent of the QIDB's net worth, whichever is the smaller.

The QIDB is governed by a board of directors and all day-to-day operations are overseen by the General Manager with the assistance of the Assistant General Manager and the Departmental Managers. The organizational structure facilitates speed of operation and accountability and is very much customer oriented.

The financial performance of the QIDB during 2001 proved to be the best in the bank's history. There was a significant increase over the previous year in sanctions, disbursements, placements and profit. The net income for the year was QR10.04 million (US$2.75 million) compared to QR8.5 million (US$2.3 million) for 1999, indicating a healthy increase of 18 per cent and earnings per share of QR0.5. As at the end of 2001, outstanding loans granted to projects, net of provisions, amounted to QR28.90 million (US$7.92 million), up from QR23.6 million (US$6.5 million) recorded at the end of the previous year.

Operations are expected to increase significantly in the coming years and, to enable smooth and efficient conduct of the anticipated increased business, the QIDB is in the process of constructing its own spacious office building, which will be ready by the end of 2002.

The QIDB is interested in investing in all industrial sectors, depending upon the merit of any given project and its potential. It has financed several projects in the chemical, construction, food and beverage, furniture and fixtures, machinery and equipment, metal, paper, textiles and other sectors. With the availability of an increasing number of petrochemical and many other products as raw materials and feedstock, the economy offers an ideal springboard for many further projects.

The QIDB is committed to playing a leading role in the indust-rialization of the country and has drawn up ambitious plans to strengthen and diversify its activities to meet the challenges that lie ahead. It aims to provide all possible assistance to investors as a 'one-stop shop' and to fulfil its primary objective of making Qatar an industrial nation to the ultimate benefit of all its citizens.

Doha Securities Market (DSM)

Dr Ghanim AlHammadi, General Manager, Doha Securities Market, Doha, Qatar

Introduction

The establishment of the Doha Securities Market (DSM) was one of the major steps aimed at consolidating the financial and economic structure of Qatar through realization of the following targets:

- formulation of a market structure to serve the country's economic development plans and to help in the fulfilment of the government's socio-economic policies;

- development and organization of the procedures to be followed in the trading of stocks in the country;

- provision of the best training for the market's employees and brokers and encouragement of the drive towards Qatarization;

- development of investor awareness and the effective dissemination of information;

- participation in the efforts being made to improve the investment climate in Qatar by helping to attract more foreign investment into the country;

- helping to amend legislation so as to permit investment in the local stock market by non-Qataris.

Background

The DSM was established by Law Decree No. 14 of 1995 – the Commercial Law of the State of Qatar – and commenced operations on 26 May 1997. At the outset, trading was undertaken manually and subsequently became semi-electronic with the accomplishment of the central registration project. It is expected that the DSM will become fully electronic upon implementation of the electronic trading project during the first quarter of 2002.

Administration and operation

A special committee named the Market Committee, which is appointed by the Council of Ministers to serve for three years, is charged with responsibility for the administration of the market and the regulation of its activities.

Eight brokers, four of which are banks, have been licensed to trade on the DSM.

In early 2001, the government extended financial support to the DSM.

Listed companies

When the DSM commenced operations in early 1997, 17 companies were listed, a number that had increased to 18 by the year end. This number then rose to 23 by 31 December 2001.

In order to be listed on the DSM, a company must have at least 100 shareholders and a minimum capital of QR10 million (US$2.74 million), a minimum of 50 per cent of which must be paid up. Once listed, companies must publish their audited financial statements annually and report their results every six months.

Market capitalization

At the inauguration of the DSM, the total capitalization of the quoted companies was estimated at QR6 billion (US$1.64 billion). By the end of 2001, market capitalization had risen to QR26.7 billion (US$7.32 billion).

Table 5.5.1 Companies listed on the DSM

Banking sector

Al-Ahli Bank
Commercial Bank of Qatar
Doha Bank
Qatar International Islamic Bank
Qatar Islamic Bank
Qatar National Bank

Insurance sector

Al-Khaleej Insurance
Doha Insurance Company
Qatar General Insurance & Reinsurance Company
Qatar Insurance Company
Qatar Islamic Insurance Company

Service sector

Al-Ahli Hospital
Al-Salam International Investment
Qatar Cinema & Film Distribution Company
Qatar Electricity & Water Company (QEWC)
Qatar Leisure & Tourism Development Company
Qatar National Navigation & Transportation Company
Qatar Real Estate Investment Company
Qatar Shipping Company
Qatar Telecommunications Company (Q-Tel)

Industry sector

Qatar Flour Mills Company
Qatar Industrial Manufacturing Company
Qatar National Cement Company

Source: Doha Securities Market

Market/price index

The DSM Price Index was launched on 1 January 1998 with a base level of 100. By the end of that year, the index had risen to 135.13, although exactly one year later it had experienced a slight fall to 134.10, which was followed by a further fall by the end of 2000, when it stood at 123.33.

2001 proved to be a better year however, as the market rose to 169.22 by 31 December, subsequently rising further during the third week of January 2002 to the highest point in the DSM's history, when it hit 176.12.

Table 5.5.2 DSM index: highs and lows, 1998–2002

	1998	1999	2000	2001	2002
High	143.04	138.84	133.18	169.22	176.12
Low	102.78	124.89	115.13	117.05	165.34

Source: Doha Securities Market

Trading figures

Before the DSM opened, the annual traded value of stocks in Qatar had been estimated at some QR320 million (US$87.7 million). For two years following the opening of the DSM, trading increased year on year, first to QR970 million (US$265.8 million) in 1998 and then to QR1.2 billion (US$328.8 million) the following year. In 2000, the value of trading declined to QR869 million (US$238.1 million), but saw a marked increase again in 2001 when the figure reached its highest in the DSM's short life at QR1.5 billion (US$411.0 million).

Table 5.5.3 Value of shares traded by sector (QR million)

	1997	1998	1999	2000	2001
Banking	149.6	636.8	608.2	299.1	609.3
Services	66.8	220.5	452.2	474.2	766.7
Industry	17.2	61.9	114.2	60.7	62.9
Insurance	13.5	50.5	57.6	34.9	64.8
Total	**247.1**	**969.8**	**1232.2**	**868.9**	**1,503.7**

Source: Doha Securities Market

Investment regulations

A new law has been issued which permits GCC (Gulf Cooperation Council) citizens to invest in the industrial and service sectors on the DSM (excluding banks and financial companies) to a maximum of 25 per cent of any company's capital. At this time, non-Qataris are only allowed to invest in Q-Tel shares, but a process is in hand to allow foreigners, initially probably only foreign residents of Qatar, to invest in local shares through mutual funds.

Part Six

Establishing Trading Links with Qatar

Living and Working in Qatar

Philip Keating

I had actually heard of Qatar well before I came to live here; however, most people do not have that advantage. It was in 1974 when I learnt about the existence of the country, a generally unknown peninsula of land jutting into the Gulf. As a tyro fighter pilot, I was struggling to get to grips with the intricacies of a single-seat Hunter. My course-mate was a Qatari Air Force lieutenant who, as it happened, came from Doha – therefore, I had a head-start on most people who had never heard of this small Gulf State. At least I could spell it. Little did I know then that 25 years later I would meet Hamed again, only this time we would be reminiscing in the quieter and more soporific surroundings of a fishing boat off Doha and not trying to shoot each other down with cine film at 20,000 feet over Anglesey.

I digress however. It just so happens that throughout my military career I have had to pack up every two or three years and move house. As befits a wandering minstrel, I have lived in some pretty awful places but also some rather memorable ones. As I come towards the end of my active service, I can honestly say that Qatar is very near the top of my list as one of the better places to have lived.

My first, more recent, glimpse of Qatar was from a Gulf Air flight from Abu Dhabi. I had been living in the United Arab Emirates for three years and my family thought that they had died and gone to heaven there. With the end of my tour in sight, and the prospect of a Doha posting, all my brood were sad to leave the penthouse apartment with a sea view and wondered what more Qatar could possibly have to offer them. I shared their sentiments completely and immediately looked up Qatar in the

Lonely Planet guide. I was far from impressed: out of all the Gulf States, the guide reckoned that there were only a few days' worth of entertainment in the capital of Doha at best. It even implied that a traveller might be advised to miss it out completely if time was short. Not a good start for us! However, before I feigned a rare illness that would guarantee repatriation, I thought we would give Qatar a chance to redeem this view, which is how we came to take a flight there one very sunny Thursday morning.

First impressions from the air are good. The seafront corniche in Doha is spectacular, with a sweeping horseshoe of gardens and palm trees seven kilometres long surrounding a small desert island – Palm Tree Island. A wonderful setting, only lacking Captain Hook's galleon moored by Pizza Hut at the 4-kilometre point. Once on the ground, however, the visage of fantasy falls rapidly away immediately on exiting the airport. Like several other places in the Gulf, many of the streets look like a permanent untidy building site but nothing that a good sergeant major and a gang of pioneers would not fail to sort out. That said, there is a wonderful impression of space over most of the city and its surrounds and, unlike Dubai or Bahrain, there is a propensity of one- or two-storey buildings unhindered by modern high-rise blocks – although that too is changing.

Of the total population of some half a million – one-fifth of which is Qatari – most live in or around Doha. Beyond the city environs there is, frankly, not much going on. Living in Doha can be quite claustrophobic for some and with a British expatriate community of over 4,000, nothing much gets missed by the grapevine of social intelligence. As to the weather, the winters are pleasant but the summers can be extremely hot and humid and most of the population wisely decamps to Europe to escape the July and August heat.

Shopping will, of course, be high on the agenda for half the family. Three years ago, my wife needed to visit about six mini-markets to garner sufficient food for one dinner party. That has now changed dramatically with the building of City Centre Doha, a huge mall many times bigger than any in Dubai. Carrefour supermarket, almost a mall in itself, has everything that the average family needs and even if the Marmite and Weetabix ship is late arriving, there are generally enough stocks in between consignments to satisfy demand. In the new Landmark Mall, Marks & Spencer and BHS are in evidence, which means that, overall, the quality and quantity of shopping is improving daily.

For the other half of the family, sport plays a significant part in expatriate living. The international 'green' golf course is second to none, with an adjacent nine-hole academy course for people like me to plough – even at night. Water sports and health clubs are naturally plentiful, even more so since the opening of the Intercontinental Hotel and the even newer Ritz Carlton resort hotel. You cannot miss the visually impressive Doha Sheraton – a grand pyramid-shaped building guarding the north end of the corniche – which has an enviable seafront location and is used by the Red Arrows aerobatic team as a focal point for their display. If you cannot find a decent spot in Doha to chill out, there is something radically wrong with you. If chilling is not for you, however, more active activities may include boating or dune bashing in a 4x4 to the south of the country. Here, half an hour from Doha, the dunes are fabulous and a journey to the Inland Sea – a natural sea incursion near the Saudi border – is a popular weekend pastime and well worth the effort.

For the other amenities and trivia that a partner might ask about, health facilities are excellent and for a small fee you are issued with a health card that allows you to use public health facilities. In addition, there are many private clinics that offer first-class facilities. There are English curriculum schools for all ages and Doha College has an excellent reputation for gaining Oxbridge and other British university places. There are plenty of expatriate clubs and societies to join, but with Doha's superb community spirit most entertainment tends to be home-based. If you get to know the Defence Attaché well, you might even be invited to the join the much sought-after cocktail parties on visiting Royal Navy ships.

There is no public transport system in Qatar and thus nearly everybody buys a 4x4 or battered battle-truck of some description. There are plenty of second-hand vehicles on the market but beware of the good-looking ones with new paint jobs and sand-blasted underside. Driving in Qatar bears a close resemblance to stock-car racing and, as with most Gulf traffic, you will be lucky to escape without a scrape on your car at some stage in your tour. Duelling Landcruisers and weaving Nissans fight for pole position at roundabouts, and traffic signals all have a red light in the sequence but I have no idea why! If you are a nervous driver, taking a taxi may be the better option, although it is not a very elegant way of arriving at an Embassy reception. There are plenty of cheap taxis that can be hailed in the street, but for comfort and style you can phone for a Doha limousine – minus the taxi dents – for a few riyals more. In addition, if you are a mum out shopping with your children you can hire a limo by the hour for an easier journey.

Air transport serves Qatar quite well and the national carrier, Qatar Airways, has many inter-Gulf flights and a daily service to London. There was a time years ago when I travelled to London on a Qatar Airways 747. It was like sitting down in my grandmother's parlour but without the smell of mothballs – comfy, worn seats with threadbare carpets and a friendly hostess offering tea and sandwiches. Nowadays, the fleet consists of shiny new Airbuses and the tea has been replaced by a wider range of beverages that would appeal to the football hooligan. Of course, British Airways and Gulf Air fly to and from Doha as well, so I would be very surprised if you were unable to find a convenient flight to take little Johnny back to boarding school.

Housing is relatively good compared to other Gulf States and generally you get more space for your money here than elsewhere. Unlike my smallish Abu Dhabi apartment in a high-rise, for the same rental money we have something similar to Balmoral here, but without the trout farm. Our first house was so large that we fear that some of our guests may have been lost and never found. We eventually decided to downsize but even then the scale was large. Our transient children assume that having a pool and their own en-suite bathroom is part of normal living. Although big may be beautiful to many, maintenance can be a headache unless you happen to have a particularly good landlord who has a proper maintenance team on hand – but sadly these are almost extinct! If you are looking for trouble-free living, there are plenty of villa compounds of all price ranges that offer pool and gym facilities with regular maintenance crews.

Of course, if you live in Doha, everyone will tell you that it is '10 minutes' from everywhere – 10 minutes to the airport, 10 minutes to the hotel, 10 minutes to the shopping mall – so geography may not be a major factor in your decision to locate. Beware of heavy traffic however. In peak periods, the convenient '10 minutes' may become a tiresome half-hour or more and if you have to travel to the office every day through the various centres of Doha, it may soon become a major gripe.

Thus, what of actual living here? Everyone will have an opinion and many may disagree with me. All I can say is that living here for me has been easy compared to many other places. My teenage children can be left to go to the club on their own and I do not worry about their welfare. Try doing that in London. Certainly, in the Gulf, the Qataris are the most hospitable and friendly people I have ever come across. On my first day, I was invited to share some supper with a local family I had never clapped eyes on before – and we are now great friends. When I lived in a sprawling estate in Bath, I never met the neighbours except at Christmas. When I had a flat tyre, several Qataris pulled over to see if they could help. In the desert, the unwritten local law is to offer assistance to the idiot Landrover driver stuck in the sand who only has a plug spanner and a packet of crisps for his day trip.

What of the Lonely Planet guide? For a backpacker who wants to see Arabic culture and other Qatari-unique interests, the guide is probably correct in that Doha has very little to offer the traveller on a shoestring budget. A souk is a souk wherever you go and Doha has several poor versions and a new one with escalators and air conditioning. However, actually living here is very different from the book's impression and, with every day that passes, Doha gets better and better. Once you get under its skin, there is far more depth to the country. Sure, the newcomer will have to battle through some pretty stiff bureaucracy for months to get the right paperwork, but the battle is worth it. Whenever I am overlooking the azure blue sea, sitting by the marina at the Ritz Carlton in November, gently sipping my claret over a medium-rare steak, I generally spare a thought for my colleagues in Whitehall – but not often!

So, whatever became of my Qatari colleague during my early training days? He became chief of the Qatar Air Force and then Minister for Defence. He has retired now, but we met up recently and spent a wonderful day fishing in something the size of a frigate. We picked up our friendship as if it were 25 years earlier – talking like excited schoolboys and boasting of our different lives and the unique experiences that we have had.

Take my advice and try living here for a spell and sharing the unique experience – you will not regret it.

Setting Up Agency and Distribution Agreements

David Silver, Solicitor, Hassan A AlKhater Law Office, Doha, Qatar

There are two specific references to contracts of commercial agency in Qatari law. The first is in Chapter 2 of Book 3 of Law No. 16 of 1971 promulgating the Civil and Commercial Law of the State of Qatar (the Civil Code). The second is Law No. 4 of 1986 regulating the business of commercial agents (the Commercial Agency Law). While the Civil Code provisions deal with those particular contractual rules that are commonly associated with agency agreements, the Commercial Agency Law affords a considerable degree of protection to a registered commercial agency agreement.

Article 1 provides that the terms of the Commercial Agency Law will apply only to a registered agreement. In order to be registered, the agreement must contain an exclusive appointment, as agent and the contract must comply with the specific requirements set out in Article 2. The Law also provides that a principal may only appoint one agent for a given territory in respect of a particular product or service or range of products or services.

The effect of registration of a commercial agency agreement under the Commercial Agency Law is to prevent either party from terminating the contract without the consent of the other party except in circumstances that justify termination. The Law also gives the agent the right to claim compensation for loss of opportunity in circumstances where the agency agreement expires in accordance with its terms and the principal refuses to renew the agreement but the agent can show that his activities have resulted in a discernible success in promoting the products or services.

The Law goes on to provide that if the principal withdraws the agency agreement in circumstances other than the term of it has expired, the principal and agent agreed to cancellation of the agreement or in the opinion of the Ministry of Economy and Commerce substantial reason existed compelling the principal to cancel the agency agreement, the Ministry has the discretion to ban the importation of the commodity that was the subject of the agency. However, in practice, the Ministry has not exercised that discretion for some time. In the event of a complaint being made to it, the Ministry will usually advise the parties to the dispute to seek recourse before the Civil and Commercial Courts.

As it is not necessary to appoint a commercial agent in order to import goods or spare parts into Qatar, in the light of the terms of the Commercial Agency Law, it is important to consider carefully whether the appointment of an exclusive commercial agent is necessary before doing so. It is possible to appoint a representative in respect of any given product or service which falls short of amounting to a registrable appointment as commercial agent. Such an agreement would have the benefit of establishing a formal contractual relationship between principal and representative, which would be governed by the general rules of contract without giving rise to the potential difficulties that would result from the existence of a registered agency agreement. Furthermore, subject only to the terms of that agreement, there would be no legal impediment upon either of the principal or the representative appointing one or more distributors if either of them wishes to do so.

Part Seven

Marketing in Qatar

Advertising and the Media

Mohammed Kadoumi, Client Services Manager, Dallah Advertising Agency, Doha, Qatar

During 2001, Qatar was the venue for a number of international conventions and conferences, thus attracting worldwide media attention. As a result, the local media has gained considerable experience and has come to realize the importance of developing capabilities in order to stand side by side with international counterparts.

Today, more media vehicles than ever are available to advertisers, which has made it necessary for them to start releasing planned advertising campaigns in cooperation with professional advertising agencies.

As the advertising and media industries in Qatar strive to catch up with their peers in the region, and with a little more organization and industry regulating, so the whole scene will change and the local media will become increasingly competent.

Press

There are five daily newspapers in Qatar, three of which are Arabic and two English. The Arabic dailies are *Al Watan* (The Nation), *Al Sharq* (The East) and *Al Raya* (The Flag). The English dailies are *Gulf Times* (published by *Al Raya*) and *The Peninsula* (published by *Al Sharq*).

In general, the press is independent and self-censored. Which daily has a greater readership or circulation is not known since no media research has ever been conducted. However, given the relatively small population of Qatar, the newspaper circulation is generally considered to be low. In addition to the local dailies, many Arabic and international newspapers that cater to expatriates can be found.

Local family magazines remain in their infancy. The market depends on the magazines that are published in neighbouring countries such as Saudi Arabia and the United Arab Emirates. Other specialized magazines (ie business and IT) are imported from abroad. However, there are a few good local magazines such as *Marhaba* and *Abode*. The former is considered a tourist magazine while the latter caters to families.

Broadcast

Qatar is best known in this area for its hosting of the Al Jazeera satellite channel, a phenomenon considered a breakthrough in the world of broadcast news. Other satellite stations are available to viewers through subscription to the cable network provided by Qatar Telecommunications Company (Q-Tel, the only communications provider in Qatar).

Qatar terrestrial TV is watched mainly by a limited number of locals and Arab residents.

With regard to radio, there is a local Arabic channel and English FM. Radio Monte Carlo recently signed an agreement for retransmission from Qatar. There is little use of Qatari radio as an advertising medium as most local radio audiences tend to favour other Gulf radio stations.

Cinema

Before 2000, there were only seven cinemas, but now, with the opening of two huge shopping malls incorporating cineplexes, the number has increased to 26. These show a variety of international movies, predominantly Western and Asian, but with some Arabic films also. It is mostly tobacco companies that use cinema screens for advertising, although there is limited take-up from car distributors also.

Advertising

International and regional advertising agencies do not have branches or representative offices in Qatar since the Qatari advertising market depends heavily on those of Dubai, Bahrain and Saudi Arabia. Few agencies are depicted as professional advertising services providers. Small shops and design houses are also available and the business is open to everybody without constraint or regulation.

Advertising expenditure in Qatar is among the lowest in the GCC (Gulf Cooperation Council) countries and all international brand campaigns are planned outside Qatar and scheduled accordingly. Nevertheless, the advertising industry is expected to become more organized and more professional as large groups and international companies make moves to enter the market to open new and more professional advertising agencies.

Market Research

*Jan Stuffers, Managing Consultant,
InCite Marketing Research, Dubai,
United Arab Emirates*

Research agencies and services

Considering Qatar's relatively high GDP per capita, there are surprisingly few specialized market research agencies to choose from in the country. A couple of well-known international research agencies have their field operations in Doha, but smaller and medium-sized agencies with a strength in knowledge of local market conditions are few and far between.

With Qatar's developing economy, the number of agencies is likely to increase. With this progress, feasibility studies for new businesses – now order of the day with agencies – will be followed by mainstream marketing research examining the relationship between brands and consumers.

Qatar's somewhat modest domestic market in terms of population size encourages the business community to explore export opportunities in neighbouring countries and beyond. Hence the research agencies that do operate in Qatar extend their capabilities – either their own or through networking – into other Gulf States and even into the Levant. To research users, the convenience of working with one agency for multinational studies with the reassurance of uniform execution in all relevant countries is often preferable and more economical compared with dealing with separate agencies in each country.

'Off-the-shelf' data available from research agencies

International market research agencies have been operating in Qatar for quite some time. Continuous multi-client surveys, such as retail audits, have been available for many years. Their findings are mostly relevant to multinational manufacturing companies marketing fast-moving consumer goods (FMCG). The retail-based audits provide brand share, distribution and allied data on consumer goods and are a useful tool in monitoring the development of brands in terms of demand and retail visibility. Some manufacturing companies and advertising agencies also subscribe to tracking studies for consumer media habits in helping to optimize their advertising spend. There are other syndicated and continuous surveys operated by the leading agencies with the aim of offering regular market research data cost effectively.

All research companies in Qatar are full-service agencies offering both qualitative and quantitative expertise. Essentially, qualitative research – eg focus groups – is exploratory in nature, often used to generate ideas and to fully probe (mostly) consumer attitudes. Quantitative research adds a numeric perspective by interviewing large numbers of respondents with a structured questionnaire. Understanding is thus gained through measurement.

The leading agencies are staffed by research professionals who are well versed in mainstream market research techniques in both quantitative and qualitative disciplines. The larger international research groups offer a wide range of research models for in-depth analysis and these are primarily designed for the needs of multinational clients to monitor their brand or advertising performance.

The most common survey topics covered by agencies include:

- advertising positioning development;
- advertising concepts;
- advertising tracking;
- brand equity evaluation;
- brand switching opportunities;
- census surveys;

- consumer lifestyle;
- customer satisfaction;
- retail distribution/merchandising;
- corporate image;
- employee surveys;
- feasibility/market entry studies;
- market experiments (shop tests, test markets);
- mystery shopper surveys;
- new product development;
- packaging research;
- price sensitivity;
- product placement tests;
- usage and attitude surveys.

Practicalities

As is the case with many other Gulf States, Qatar has a sizeable expatriate population of around 70 per cent and hence research consultants must understand, respect and accommodate in their research practice the sensitivities of different lifestyles, particularly when driven by Islamic or ethnic values. Any survey that aims to represent the Qatari population at large deals with different nationalities. Qataris are an hospitable nation and this helps the researcher to find willing respondents. However, cordiality may extend into providing overly accommodating answers. The gap between what is said and what is actually done is influenced by the culture of the respondent. It is generally wider with Asians compared with Westerners. This is of particular concern when dealing with concept or feasibility studies whose aim it is to predict future behaviour. An understanding of this phenomenon is critical in the interpretation of findings when the researcher is preparing recommendations. Answers from respondents cannot always be taken at face value.

In all of the GCC countries, random sampling in quantitative research is at best difficult because the method relies on intercepting respondents freely. In Qatar, this is generally not possible with females for cultural and religious regions. Research agencies usually resort to a method based on referrals to achieve a required sample, but this inevitably leads to an inherent bias. Various techniques are used to minimize this effect but it cannot be eradicated completely. Similarly, in arranging focus groups, great care needs to be taken with the composition of respondents and the choice of the moderator. Mixing gender for Qatari groups is not only unworkable but is also considered embarrassing and therefore offensive.

Naturally, research agencies advise their clients in this respect, but companies considering research need to be aware of the parameters within which surveys in Qatar are conducted.

Importance

In general, just under 65 per cent of new businesses fail within their first three years and, according to the *Wall Street Journal*, as many as 86 per cent of new brands suffer the same fate. Listening to customers – be they prospective or existing – and adapting to their constantly changing wants and needs is critical in creating as well as maintaining excitement and demand for products or services. Market research can definitely help maximize the potential of initiatives – in whichever area of the marketing mix – or prevent costly misjudgements by bridging the perilous cleft between the marketer's perceptions and the reality of market dynamics. This applies to any idea – a new business, changing or developing new products (services), advertising, packaging etc – that demands precious investment of a company's time and capital.

Fundamental to this is obtaining accurate and relevant information. However, well-reasoned and sensible recommendations are likely to provide a better understanding than sombre statistics. Qatar's market research agencies are well equipped to provide solid guidance, but as with choosing any supplier, companies interested in conducting a survey need to ensure that the range of capabilities and credentials suit the particular need at hand.

Part Eight

Labour Issues in Qatar

Employment Law

David Silver, Solicitor, Hassan A AlKhater Law Office, Doha, Qatar

Qatar is able to boast one of the earliest employment laws in the region, Labour Law, Law No. 3 of 1962. The Law regulates contracts of employment, the working week, overtime, holidays and entitlement to sick leave, the safety, health and welfare of employees and provides for compensation for disability or death caused by industrial injury or occupational disease. The Law also regulates labour relations, limiting the rights to strike and lock-out, the right of termination of contracts of employment, and grants the Civil Court the right to order reinstatement or compensation in the event of arbitrary dismissal. In the case of foreign companies registered in Qatar, it also creates an obligation to pay end-of-service benefits to all employees having continuous service in excess of one year except in circumstances in which the employer is entitled to terminate the contract of employment summarily.

As an alternative to the obligation to pay end-of-service benefits, the Law permits an employer to establish a pension scheme for its employees, which will result in the employee receiving a net benefit greater than that to which the employee would have been entitled as end-of-service benefit. However, the employee retains discretion to choose between the pension scheme and the statutory payment. As a result, it is particularly important that foreign companies transferring employees to Qatar should review carefully the terms of the contract of employment prepared for the purposes of compliance with the Labour Law in order to identify, and to limit, to the extent possible any exposure to multiple claims in different jurisdictions arising in respect of any given employee.

It is commonly the case that foreign investors employing staff in Qatar will have a staff manual of general application setting out internal regulations by which all of its employees are expected to abide, including disciplinary procedures. Any provision contained in the manual that is contrary to the Labour Law, Law No. 3 of 1962 will be void. The imposition of disciplinary procedures and a tariff of penalties for particular offences which do not conflict with the Law is permitted subject to sufficient notice being given to the employees affected by it, and any such tariff must first be approved by the Labour Department.

All contracts of employment and other personnel records must be prepared in Arabic. Such documents may also be maintained in another language, but if so, the Arabic translation is the text of reference and in the event of a discrepancy between the two, the Arabic text will prevail.

Human Resource-related Issues

Finbarr Sexton, Ernst & Young, Doha, Qatar

Labour supply and relations

Labour supply

The workforce in Qatar consists mainly of Asian and expatriate Arab workers. There are also a significant number of European and US nationals with specialized expertise. As there is currently a shortage of Qatari labour, there is no obligation to use local workers. However, it is government policy to ensure that Qatari nationals are employed to the fullest extent possible.

In recent years, the Ministry of the Interior has imposed quotas on visa allocations for citizens of certain countries.

Labour legislation

Labour Law, Law No. 3 of 1962 and later amendments regulate employment matters.

Wages and salaries are normally agreed between the employer and employee. There is no requirement to pay employees either an annual bonus or a share of profit.

A normal working week consists of eight hours per day, six days per week. This is reduced to six hours per day during the month of Ramadan. Overtime should be paid at a minimum rate of time and a quarter (although time and a half is more usual) except on Fridays and public holidays when the minimum is time and a half.

A statutory minimum of two weeks' annual leave is due to employees with less than five years' continuous service. After this period, the minimum is four weeks per year. In practice, the amount of leave granted in a year varies considerably depending on the employer. The employer, usually being a sponsor, is liable to pay all expatriate workforce airfares to the home country on engagement and termination.

Labour relations

Trade unions are not permitted in Qatar.

Social security

There are no social insurance or other statutory deductions from pay, nor are any similar contributions required from employers. Under the Social Security Law No. 38 of 1995, the Ministry of Endowments and Islamic Affairs operates a state-funded social insurance scheme, which provides salaries to low-income Qatari nationals permanently resident in Qatar. The scheme is designed to assist widows, divorcees, low-income families, the handicapped and other welfare categories.

Payroll taxes and employee benefits

Payroll taxes

There are no payroll taxes in Qatar as individuals in employment are not liable to income tax at present.

Dismissal and severance payments

Staff may be dismissed provided the cause is reasonable and adequate notice is given. Entities in which the Qatari ownership is less than 51 per cent are required to pay severance (terminal benefit) payments when:

- the dismissal is without a cause deemed reasonable under the Labour Law;

- the contract ends and employment ceases;

- an employee resigns after more than two years' service.

The terminal benefit payment is calculated on the following basis:

- three weeks' basic pay plus cost of living allowance for each of the first five years;

- four weeks' pay for the next five years;

- five weeks' pay for the next ten years;

- six weeks' pay for each year over twenty years.

When an employee resigns before the completion of two years' service, he has no entitlement to benefit; after two years' service, the entitlement is one-third of the total benefit as calculated above; after five years' service, the entitlement is two-thirds of the total benefit; after ten years' service, he is entitled to the total benefit as calculated above.

Special requirements for foreign nationals

Gulf Cooperation Council (GCC) nationals may live and work in Qatar without obtaining special permission. Nationals of other countries must obtain residence and work permits before their entry into Qatar, except in the case of transit and visit visas.

Applications for permits are normally made through a Qatari Embassy or Consulate. They must be based on a formal offer for employment that describes the nature of the position. The Department of Immigration issues the permit, which can take a few weeks to process.

Work permits and other licences

Once an employee arrives in Qatar to take up employment, an application for a residence permit will be made to the Immigration Department by the local sponsor. These are becoming increasingly straightforward to arrange and are normally available within six weeks of arrival. Family dependants also receive residence permits under the sponsorship of the family member employed in Qatar. For long-term visitor and residence visas, it is necessary to complete various health and fingerprint examination procedures. Most companies have well-established departments to assist new arrivals in the completion of the necessary formalities.

A person employed in Qatar may not work for anyone other than his sponsor. Sponsorship cannot be transferred until an employee has worked with the original sponsor for at least two years and has been granted a release letter by that sponsor. However, it is possible for an employee to join another employer on a secondment basis with the permission of his sponsor. Secondment arrangements are allowed for six months, renewable thereafter, when the employee has completed one year of service.

There are no restrictions on the employment of women. Opportunities for such employment are determined by market demand and lie mainly in the teaching and medical professions and in accountancy and secretarial work. An employee with a residence permit may apply for a family visa where his basic salary is not less than QR4,000 and his employer provides appropriate family accommodation facilities.

Identity cards

All expatriate residents in Qatar are required to carry identify cards. These are normally obtained at the same time as residence permits.

Driving licences

All residents driving vehicles in Qatar are required to hold a valid Qatari driving licence. These are obtained after the residence permit has been issued and usually involve driving and sight tests.

Health cards

In order to receive medical treatment from polyclinics and hospitals, it is necessary for foreign residents to obtain health cards. Upon payment of a nominal fee, these are issued by the nearest polyclinic to the person's residence on production of relevant residence permits. Health cards must be shown on all polyclinic and hospital visits.

Qatarization

It is stated government policy to replace expatriate manpower with appropriately skilled Qatari staff in all government and semi-government corporations. Qatar Petroleum (QP) and its subsidiary and affiliated companies have set a target of 50 per cent Qatarization by 2005. This trend is also expected to gain momentum in the private sector as the flow of suitably qualified Qatari graduates increases. To meet the 50 per cent target, QP has developed a 'Qatarization with Quality' initiative aimed at ensuring that Qatari staff receive in-post training and development to acquire the requisite skills and experience required for their employment positions. This initiative is being adopted at varying levels by other entities.

In July 2001, the government enacted a new law, Law No. 11 of 2001 – Regulations Relating to the Practice of Engineering Professions, organizing the engineering services sector. The Law stipulates that professional engineering service entities doing business in Qatar must employ at least two Qatari qualified engineers. In the short term, the adoption of the requirements of this Law is likely to force a number of small professional services firms to either reorganize or close, as it may not be possible for these firms to meet the Qatarization requirements of the Law.

Part Nine

The Real Estate Market in Qatar

Residential Property Market

Simon King, Apollo Enterprises,
Real Estate Division, Doha, Qatar

Introduction

For companies relocating to the Arabian Gulf, Qatar is emerging as an industrial giant in the oil and gas sector of the world markets. With the influx of expatriate workers for the many upcoming projects as well as Qatar's opportunity to host the 2006 Asian Games, the country's property market is developing at a rapid pace.

As with most other Gulf States, Qatar's property market is only available to non-GCC (Gulf Cooperation Council) citizens in the rental sector. It has been rumoured for some time that, in the future, land and existing properties may be purchased by expatriates, but this has yet to come into force.

Decisions

In Qatar, a residence permit is not required in order to sign a lease. Although some people may wish to wait until their residency application has been processed, this can be a long procedure, and any delay may mean losing a 'dream home' as many landlords prefer not to wait. A more recent trend in Doha is for employees to sign a lease agreement in their own names; this is chiefly as a result of Qatar Petroleum's decision to replace its in-house housing department with a system that provides employees with monthly allowances.

The grade of the employee dictates the housing allowance; thus, a range of accommodation is available ranging from a relatively spartan property to a fully furnished all-inclusive villa. Once the budget has been established, it is decision time.

The first – and possibly most important – decision is that of selecting a competent property agent. It is essential to use a reputable agency such as Apollo Enterprises. There are many agencies in Qatar and thus it is vital to choose one with care as, by seeking the advice of several agencies, you are likely to visit the same property more than once, thus wasting valuable time.

It is essential to have answered the following questions in order to give the agent clear information regarding requirements and in turn find the most suitable property:

- Do you want a furnished or unfurnished property?

- Do you want a villa or an apartment?

- How many bedrooms and bathrooms do you want?

- Do you want to live on a compound or in an independent property?

- Do you want to live near a school?

- Do you want to live in or out of town?

Qatar has a large expatriate population that tends to be relatively widespread. There are areas that house predominantly one culture over others and a reputable agent will be able to advise upon which area is most suitable.

Lease information

Residential leases in Qatar tend to cover two years for a new or furnished property, with annual opportunities to renew for subsequent years. The initial period for which a lease is signed is usually fixed, although there are emergency release protection clauses in the Real Estate Law, Law No. 2 of 1975 concerning the Lease of Premises and Builidngs, for special cases. Both tenant and landlord have a two-month notice period before the end of a lease to state their intentions. It is very uncommon for a landlord to attempt to increase the monthly rent. Once the lease has been signed (and stamped in the case of a company lease), both parties retain an original copy of the lease. Agents may ask for a copy for future reference.

Payment terms

Payment terms vary widely in Qatar. The larger compounds prefer either bi-annual or quarterly payments, although on occasion landlords have asked for the full year's rent in advance. This is generally applicable to company lettings. With the new trend of monthly allowances taking effect, an increasing number of landlords are accepting monthly post-dated cheques on a year-in-advance basis. This still gives them the equivalent of a year's rent as failure to honour a cheque in Qatar can have serious consequences. The agent will help negotiate the best payment terms as each landlord has his own requirements.

The majority of landlords ask for a refundable deposit. Although this can be up to a maximum of two months' rent, it is more usually one month. Furnished properties almost always require a deposit.

Additional costs

In addition to rent deposits, there is also a QR2,000 (US$550) deposit to be lodged with the Qatar General Electricity and Water Corporation, which is refundable on vacation of the property and once a tenant's accounts have been settled. The cost per unit for utilities is: electricity QR0.06 (US$0.016); water QR4.4 (US$1.205).

When applying for an international telephone line, a guarantor in the form of either a sponsor or employer/company is required. As an alternative, residents can lodge a deposit of QR1,000 (US$275). The same applies for a dedicated mobile or Internet connection. With regard to mobile phones, there is a 'pay as you go' system available which is initially quicker and cheaper to obtain as no paperwork or documentation is required. It should be noted that at present no call charges are levied for local calls made using a landline to another landline (ie not to or from a mobile).

General information

With regard to the maintenance of the property, the landlord is responsible for any major structural, electrical or plumbing work required. This issue should be discussed during the contract preparations and should be included in the lease.

Those wishing to decorate the property should gain the landlord's approval before undertaking work. Some landlords will insist that the property be returned to its original condition at the end of the lease, with fair wear and tear acceptable as stated by the lease agreement. Failure to comply with this may lead to deductions from the deposit for repainting. It is important, therefore, to always gain the landlord's approval before embarking on any work that will dramatically change the property.

Should a property with its own private pool be required, it is advisable to check if the landlord has a contract with a reputable company covering maintenance and upkeep that can be continued. If this is not the case, the agent may be able to assist in locating such a company. The cost to carry out maintenance personally will be in the region of QR500–QR750 (US$140–US$210) for an average-sized garden pool.

Occasionally, landlords provide properties with satellite television, but in most cases installation costs will be borne by the tenant. There are several systems to choose from, but the most popular will cost in the region of QR250 (US$70) for installation with a monthly subscription of QR260 (US$73).

Commercial Property Market

Simon King, Apollo Enterprises,
Real Estate Division, Doha, Qatar

During the early 1980s, Doha had very little in terms of dedicated office space. Many firms used large residential properties and simply adapted them for their needs. This practice is still very popular today as one can acquire a large property with a sizeable floor area for a considerable amount less than that same floor area would cost in an office block. This is becoming more difficult, however, as the government has recently been re-zoning areas to be purely residential, thus forcing businesses to move to newer, dedicated office buildings.

With many companies expanding their interests as a result of rapid developments in the oil and gas sector, there is an increased demand for quality space. This has led to an increase in the market price however. Until recently, Doha had very few quality office blocks, but with several recent completions, and with many more underway, the West Bay end of the corniche will soon have risen to new heights. At present, many government departments are moving to occupy these developments as there has been little interest from the private sector due to high rental rates.

An increasing number of landowners are developing mid-sized properties as this enables them to compete with the established residential properties as they can offer new, top-quality premises at only slightly increased rates.

The opening of the regional office of the Gulf Business Centre in Doha in 2001 has enabled a great number of companies to establish themselves in Doha. The Gulf Business Centre's flexible all-inclusive package allows companies to operate without the organizational hassles of setting up a fully functioning office or finding premises.

With availability in a wide range of commercial properties, the Doha market can fulfil any requirements set. However, consultation with a reputable agency will ensure the best rental terms and a wider selection of property.

Leases

The wide range of requirements varying from client to client means that there are no standard lease formats. The majority of leases are short term of between one and three years.

It is common for owners to be open to negotiation regarding terms and conditions for secondary and tertiary space; however, prime buildings tend to have set rents and rental periods.

Payment terms

Payment terms are dependent upon the owner. In general, secondary and tertiary space is payable either quarterly in advance or by post-dated cheques. Prime space will usually require a minimum of quarterly payments and some may require bi-annual payments. On rare occasions it has been known for owners to try to press for a full year in advance. This is usually when the client wishes to negotiate a heavy reduction in the rent.

Service charges

Service charges are likely to be levied by owners of tower space or malls. The charge will usually cover the maintenance of the building, security and cleaning of any common areas, in addition to the running costs and general repairs to air conditioning systems.

It is wise to clarify with the owner whether the service charge will cover consumption of electricity and water, or if there will be individual tenant meters.

Fitting out

A rent-free period for fitting out an office (and the subsequent length of this period) is dependent upon the negotiating skills of the agent.

Owners of secondary and tertiary space are very reluctant to allow a rent-free period at the beginning of a lease. Owners of prime space may agree to a rent-free period, as larger companies occupying these areas tend to require a sizeable amount of preparatory work. A reputable agent will be able to supply a list of specialist companies and other construction companies in Doha capable of carrying out any required work.

Termination

Should a client not wish to renew a lease, in most cases it is necessary to inform the landlord in writing at least 60 days before the expiry of the lease.

Should early termination become necessary, several options are available: if the company is ceasing all operations in Qatar, it is common practice for landlords to accept 60 days' notice for vacating the premises; for any other reason, it is at the landlord's discretion to allow the termination either by securing a replacement tenant or by means of a penalty payment.

Renewal clauses in leases commonly state that the same terms and conditions will apply. Rent reviews are generally by negotiation and reflect market conditions. It is not common for rent increases to occur.

Once the premises have been vacated, the landlord will usually insist on an inspection and, in the case of damage which is not deemed normal wear and tear, will inform the tenant what is required to return the premises to a condition similar to that at the date of occupation.

Parking

Car ownership is high throughout the Gulf. This, combined with the common practice of supplying the minimum number of parking spaces required by law, leaves many companies with a problem regarding sufficient, secure staff parking. Leases often state the number of parking spaces that will be provided and this is usually relative to the size of the premises. If a larger number of spaces is required, it is necessary to ensure that the increased entitlement is included in the lease.

Insurance

As part of the lease agreement, the landlord is responsible for the insurance of the building, while the tenant is responsible for the insurance of the office contents. Should it not be stated in the lease, check with the landlord as to what each party's responsibilities are.

Rental trends

Rates are usually quoted on a square metre basis although lease agreements do state floor area and total monthly or annual costs.

Agency fees

In Qatar, it is common practice for the landlord to meet any agency fees for introducing a tenant to his property, whether commercial or residential.

Part Ten

General Aspects of
Business Culture

Cross-cultural Considerations for Life and Business in Qatar

Jeremy Williams OBE, Handshaikh Ltd, and author of 'Don't They Know it's Friday'

Your company has offered you the appointment of resident company representative in Doha. Where do you start to learn about Qatar? Start here before you lose yourself in 'fact finding' and miss the main point that it is 'people' and 'relationships' that matter most in Qatar.

First, clear your mind of misconceptions about Arab geography and terminology. The western boundary of 'the Middle East' is usually regarded to be that between Libya and Egypt, while 'the Gulf' comprises the six Gulf Cooperation Council (GCC) countries of Kuwait, Saudi Arabia, Bahrain, Qatar, the United Arab Emirates and the Sultanate of Oman. Take care with the expressions 'the Arabian Gulf' and 'the Persian Gulf' since the shoreline is shared between Arabia and Iran (Persia). The inhabitants of Iran are not Arabs, nor Semitic; they are Indo-Europeans whose tongue is Farsi, not Arabic. Arabic, of course, is the language of the Muslim world – which spreads far beyond the bounds of 'the Middle East' or 'the Arab World'. The latter consists generally of three areas: the Northern (or Levantine) region, North Africa, and the Arabian Peninsula and Gulf States. Some commentators find that the categories of rich/poor, old/new and stable/unstable, malevolent/benevolent dictatorships are useful divisions for grouping the countries of the Arab World.

Second, and importantly, do not give much credence to those who, having lived for a number of years in one part of the region, eg Kuwait, now offer to advise you on Qatar because they 'know all about the Arabs' since 'Arabs are all the same'. They do not have personal experience of the part of the Arab world in which you are now interested (ie Qatar) and 'part' is the significant word here, nation is not really good enough since there are differences within the Gulf countries themselves. Thus, do your homework on your part of the Arab world and do not mentally group it with other parts. Learn, for example, the facts of Qatar's enormous gas fields and its cautious plans for exploiting its good fortune in the future. Recognize that Qatar is the Gulf's next success story, but note its hope not to change its character overmuch in the future. Qatar seeks to 'make haste slowly' – to learn from its already-rich Gulf neighbours in terms of the effect that vast wealth can have on Arab and Muslim heritage, particularly the latter. Qatar hopes to balance between the benefits and disadvantages of moving from being a relatively poor Gulf State to one of its richest (per capita) in the next few years.

Third, the expression 'the Arabs' is as unhelpful a demographic expression as 'the Europeans'. Some similarity may exist internally within each grouping in terms of political systems or religion for example (eg Islam, an essential ingredient within the Arab world), but it is never wise to regard those who form 'the Arabs' (or 'the Europeans') as though they have the same personal characteristics. People are different everywhere. What is normal behaviour for you may be wholly abnormal behaviour elsewhere.

Your company has been sensible and has paid for you and your spouse to spend a week in Qatar some months before you are due to take up residence. You have assembled the facts that really matter to a family: schooling; housing; travel; and visas. Things are looking good. You have met someone who says he hopes to be your sponsor (see below), who is charming and knows all about your company and its expectations. Your children are excited at the prospect of living abroad. Your spouse is content. You know what your company expects of you and you have a decent line manager to whom you report at head office. Both of you have worked well together before. You are reasonably content with the allowances and emoluments that will affect you and your family at your new destination. The goods and services that your company offers sell well to the rest of the world and thus the Gulf will be much the same (presumably). You have high standards and high expectations. You now want the job. You are keen. You can apply the same marketing techniques in the Gulf as any-where else. What could possibly go wrong?

You have only scratched the surface of the situation. Now address the 'hassle factor', the 'personal' and the 'personnel' elements. Do you have any idea of the way in which Arab nationals actually conduct their business? Does your head office really have the arrogance to believe that its own standards, habits and methods will simply 'read across' to the Gulf? Why would that be? What presumption! Even though Qatar – and the other Gulf countries generally – have had considerable exposure to the West (mainly from the United Kingdom previously, but now from the United States), it has its own methods of reaching decisions, and these are methods that may seem wholly illogical to you and your head office, but are nevertheless perfectly effective in Qatar.

Focus urgently on your sponsor. Do you understand what 'sponsor' means in Qatari terms? Does your company understand that a relationship with a 'sponsor' is effectively a 'Catholic marriage' because severance is not normally possible regardless of the performance of the individuals concerned on either side? The selection of the company sponsor is the single most important act of any company new to Qatar (or to the Gulf generally). Who is he? Who knows him? What is his reputation? Who else has offered his services as your company sponsor? Has any relation-ship between your company and a sponsor been decided? Who in your company has been involved in the process? Do you trust that person's judgement in terms of his or her exposure to Gulf Arabs and the importance of the subject? Has an agreement act-ually been signed? Be clear and robust on this next point: if there is the slightest doubt in your mind that the process of sponsor selection has been handled casually by your company, and if – fortunately – there is no agreement in place, demand that your company delays closure until the whole subject has been closely examined and approved at Board level. If an agreement is already in place, ensure that your line manager at home understands the details of the relationship and the risks involved.

Gulf law, regulations and practice are generally very much on the side of the Gulf national and national company. Outside certain Free Zones, all companies are owned or controlled by Gulf nationals or Gulf companies; exclusive foreign ownership is as good as unknown, although some opportunities for 99-year leases are being granted in the United Arab Emirates, and Bahrain does permit 100 per cent foreign ownership for specified types of company. Increasingly, young Gulf Arabs (50 per cent of the GCC countries' population is under 15 years old) are expecting employment by right and their laws demand – for good reason – that all companies take on more nationals. 'Qatarization' is a central, firm requirement of the Qatari government and this demand on foreign companies operating in Qatar must be kept in mind at all times. Many nationals – who form the minority of Gulf populations – are excellent employees (and managers), but many come from a family where great wealth has been the norm for perhaps two generations. The 'work ethic' has therefore not been a prominent Gulf Arab characteristic nor has 'good timekeeping' – always a favourite cross-cultural subject noted by Westerners whose watches and diaries usually dominate their lifestyle. However, in Qatar, such traits have yet to develop fully since personal wealth has not been at the same level as in other Gulf countries; it may be that young Qataris can find full, natural, un-enforced employment without difficulty since the Qatari has always known that personal effort and contribution has been needed.

The problems of gaining access to local decision-takers will come to govern your endeavours in the Gulf. It will be essential that you have a genuine friend at head office who understands the way of life of the Gulf. You need protection from those back home who believe that you have somehow, in Western terms, 'gone funny' – for example, you cannot even accomplish the simplest of tasks, such as obtaining from the customer a straight answer to a straight question, or obtaining a timely programme for the CEO's Gulf visit. Without such a friend, your stature in head office may well plummet and your promotion prospects may suffer unfairly since your former colleagues have no idea of what you are undergoing, or how to judge it. 'I managed to speak to Shaikh Abdullah in private for five minutes today about our project. I'm very happy. He said he would think about it all' might be a remark you might make in innocence on the telephone to head office, but such a remark will only confirm to many there that you really have become 'odd', whereas the remark should have demonstrated that you have managed to gain the most respectable access to a most powerful person. You are not 'odd' at all; you deserve the highest congratulation from the Board. To gain access needs good luck and good exposure to, and understanding of, local practice. 'Access' is the key to everything in the Gulf. It takes time and effort to achieve.

Things are different in the Gulf. Things can happen very quickly after perhaps months or years of waiting. Once an important person has focused on a topic, instructions are given that cause actions to occur that can astound Western expatriates by both their speed and their nature. Gulf Arabs are dismayed that others – Westerners – cannot behave with the same flexibility and speed as they can. The solution is to understand the 'culture' of 'your' part of the Gulf, ie Qatar, and to have the grace and personality to adapt to it accordingly.

Material things – housing, hotels, swimming pools etc – are usually more than satisfactory; this is not the main point to bear in mind when considering employment in the Gulf. The mental stresses and strains must be discovered since it is these that can ruin careers and break marriages. Thus, do your homework on more than just the 'facts' of Qatar; look behind these to the more important cross-cultural factors and decide if you have the character (and company back-up and funding) to stay the pace. Pack patience and resilience in your hold baggage and happily pay the excess baggage charge for these two essential Gulf items.

Memo to all HR departments: Do not send impatient people to the Gulf. If there is no choice, then start the re-selection process again ready for about a year's time. This is about when the current – impatient – incumbent will blow up and have to be replaced.

Finally, 11 September 2001. The long-term effects of the tragedies in the United States in terms of their international impact are, with one exception, unclear. In terms of preparing, as a Westerner for life or business in the Gulf, the exception is the overwhelming need to study the facts of Islam. Qatar is a cautious and wholly Islamic state. Westerners are usually ignorant – perhaps fearful – of Islam and this lack of Western knowledge of a great religion has become dangerous and open to abuse.

Part Eleven

Appendices

Appendix I:
Useful Addresses

Chamber of Commerce and Industry

Qatar Chamber of Commerce and Industry
PO Box 402
Doha
Qatar
Tel: (+974) 462 1131
Fax: (+974) 462 1908

Ministries and Business-related Government Agencies

Ministry of Finance
PO Box 3322
Doha
Qatar
Tel: (+974) 446 1444, 441 3366
Fax: (+974) 443 6959, 441 4418

Ministry of Economy and Commerce
PO Box 22355
Doha
Qatar
Tel: (+974) 443 2103
Fax: (+974) 443 1412

Ministry of Energy and Industry
PO Box 2599
Doha
Qatar
Tel: (+974) 483 2121
Fax: (+974) 483 2024

Qatar Central Bank (QCB)
PO Box 1234
Doha
Qatar
Tel: (+974) 445 6456
Fax: (+974) 443 0490

Department of Industrial Development (DID)
PO Box 2599
Doha
Qatar
Tel: (+974) 483 2121
Fax: (+974) 483 2024

Qatar General Electricity and Water Corporation (QGEWC)
PO Box 41
Doha
Qatar
Tel: (+974) 432 6622
Fax: (+974) 444 0048

Qatar Petroleum Corporation (QP)
PO Box 3212
Doha
Qatar
Tel: (+974) 449 1491
Fax: (+974) 483 1125

Central Tenders Committee
PO Box 1908
Doha
Qatar
Tel: (+974) 441 3098, 441 4265
Fax: (+974) 443 0250

Planning Council
PO Box 1855
Doha
Qatar
Tel: (+974) 444 4141
Fax: (+974) 442 5555

Qatar Industrial Development Bank (QIDB)
PO Box 22789
Doha
Qatar
Tel: (+974) 442 1600
Fax: (+974) 431 7730

Embassies

France
PO Box 2669
Doha
Qatar
Tel: (+974) 483 2283
Fax: (+974) 483 2254

Germany
PO Box 3064
Doha
Qatar
Tel: (+974) 487 6959
Fax: (+974) 487 6949

Italy
PO Box 4188
Doha
Qatar
Tel: (+974) 466 7842
Fax: (+974) 466 4644

Japan
PO Box 2208
Doha
Qatar
Tel: (+974) 483 1224
Fax: (+974) 483 2178

United Kingdom
PO Box 3
Doha
Qatar
Tel: (+974) 442 1991, 435 3543 (Commercial Section)
Fax: (+974) 443 8692, 435 6131 (Commercial Section)

United States of America
PO Box 2399
Doha
Qatar
Tel: (+974) 488 4101
Fax: (+974) 488 4298

Airport

Doha International Airport
Tel: (+974) 462 2999 (Flight Information)
Tel: (+974) 465 6666 (Airport PABX)

Hotels

Sheraton Doha Hotel and Resort
PO Box 6000
Doha
Qatar
Tel: (+974) 485 4444, 483 3833
Fax: (+974) 483 2323
E-mail: sherdoha@qatar.net.qa

Doha Marriott Gulf Hotel
PO Box 1911
Doha
Qatar
Tel: (+974) 443 2432
Fax: (+974) 441 8784
E-mail: marriott@qatar.net.qa

Ramada Hotel
PO Box 1768
Doha
Qatar
Tel: (+974) 441 7417
Fax: (+974) 441 0941
E-mail: ramada@qatar.net.qa

Hotel Intercontinental Doha
PO Box 6822
Doha
Qatar
Tel: (+974) 484 4444
Fax: (+974) 483 9555
E-mail: doha@interconti.im

The Ritz Carlton Doha
PO Box 2977
Doha
Qatar
Tel: (+974) 485 7713
Fax: (+974) 483 7660
E-mail: rcdoha@qatar.net.qa

Car Hire (Doha International Airport)

Avis Rent A Car
Tel: (+974) 462 2180
E-mail: avis@qatar.net.qa

Budget Car and Van Rental
Tel: (+974) 462 2678
E-mail: budget@qatar.net.qa

Hertz
Tel: (+974) 462 2563

Business Services

Accountants and Auditors

Ernst & Young
PO Box 164
Doha
Qatar
Tel: (+974) 441 4599
Fax: (+974) 441 4649
E-mail: eydoha@qatar.net.qa

KPMG Peat Marwick
PO Box 4473
Doha
Qatar
Tel: (+974) 432 9698
Fax: (+974) 442 5626
E-mail: kpmgpm@qatar.net.qa

Arthur Andersen & Co
PO Box 15148
Doha
Qatar
Tel: (+974) 483 8241
Fax: (+974) 483 8245

Deloitte & Touche
PO Box 431
Doha
Qatar
Tel: (+974) 442 2168
Fax: (+974) 442 2131
E-mail: dtmedoha@qatar.net.qa

PricewaterhouseCoopers
PO Box 6689
Doha
Qatar
Tel: (+974) 441 5700
Fax: (+974) 441 6040

Advertising Agencies

Dallah Advertising Agency
PO Box 8545
Doha
Qatar
Tel: (+974) 444 1409
Fax: (+974) 444 7793
E-mail: dallahaa@qatar.net.qa

Property Consultants/Real Estate Agents

Apollo Enterprises
Real Estate Division
PO Box 2032
Doha
Qatar
Tel: (+974) 468 9522
Fax: (+974) 468 9621
E-mail: apollo@qatar.net.qa

Legal Consultants

Hassan A AlKhater Law Office
PO Box 1737
Doha
Qatar
Tel: (+974) 443 7770
Fax: (+974) 443 7772

Insurance Services

Qatar Insurance Company
PO Box 666
Doha
Qatar
Tel: (+974) 449 0443
Fax: (+974) 483 1569
E-mail: qatarins@qatar.net.qa

Management Consultancy (Business Development & Marketing: Business-to-Business)

The Philip Dew Consultancy Limited
PO Box 11836
Bahrain
Tel: (+973) 790886
Fax: (+973) 790729
E-mail: pdew@batelco.com.bh

Management Consultancy (Marketing: Business-to-Business)

ASA Consulting
PO Box 238
The Ridings
Cobham
Surrey KT11 2WP
United Kingdom
Tel: (+44) 1372 844317
Fax: (+44) 1372 844437
E-mail: asaconsult@btinternet.com

Appendix II: Contributors' Contact Details

Abu-Ghazaleh Intellectual Property
TMP Agents
PO Box 2620
Doha
Qatar
Tel: (+974) 441 6455
Fax: (+974) 442 5687
E-mail: agiptmp@qatar.net.qa

Apollo Enterprises
PO Box 2032
Doha
Qatar
Tel: (+974) 468 9522 (Property Division)
Fax: (+974) 468 9521
E-mail: apollo@qatar.net.qa

ASA Consulting
PO Box 238
The Ridings
Cobham
Surrey KT11 2WP
United Kingdom
Tel: (+44) 1372 844317
Fax: (+44) 1372 844437
E-mail: asaconsult@btinternet.com

David Chaddock
E-mail: chaddock@iee.org

Commercial Bank of Qatar QSC
PO Box 3232
Doha
Qatar
Tel: (+974) 449 0000
Fax: (+974) 449 0067
Website: http://www.cbq.com.qa

Dallah Advertising
PO Box 8545
Doha
Qatar
Tel: (+974) 444 4522
Fax: (+974) 444 7793
E-mail: dallahaa@qatar.net.qa

Doha Securities Market
PO Box 22114
Doha
Qatar
Tel: (+974) 432 9865, 432 8025
Fax: (+974) 432 6497

Ernst & Young
PO Box 164
Al-Abdulghani Tower
Airport Road
Doha
Qatar
Tel: (+974) 441 4599
Fax: (+974) 441 4649
Website: http://www.ey.com/eyme

Handshaikh Ltd
PO Box 123
Alresford
Hampshire SO24 0ZF
United Kingdom

Tel: (+44) 1962 771699
Fax: (+44) 1962 771814
Tel: (+971 4) 351 7624 (Dubai)
Fax: (+971 4) 352 1033 (Dubai)
E-mail: mail@handshaikh.com
Website: http://www.handshaikh.com

Hassan A AlKhater Law Office
PO Box 1737
Doha
Qatar
Tel: (+974) 443 7770
Fax: (+974) 443 7772
E-mail: haklegal@qatar.net.qa

Incite Marketing Research
PO Box 62011
Dubai
United Arab Emirates
Tel: (+974) 332 6327
Fax: (+974) 332 8388
E-mail: incite@emirates.net.ae

Gordon MacKenzie
General Manager
Ramada Hotel
PO Box 1768
Doha
Qatar
Tel: (+974) 441 7417
Fax: (+974) 441 0941
E-mail: ramada@qatar.net.qa

Philip Dew Consultancy Limited
PO Box 11836
Bahrain
Tel: (+973) 790886
Fax: (+973) 790729
E-mail: pdew@batelco.com.bh

Qatar Industrial Development Bank (QIDB)
PO Box 22789
Doha
Qatar
Tel: (+974) 442 1600
Fax: (+974) 435 0433
Website: http://www.qidb.com

Qatar Insurance Company
PO Box 666
Doha
Qatar
Tel: (+974) 449 0443
Fax: (+974) 483 1569
E-mail: qatarins@qatar.net.qa

Index

Other titles in this series from Kogan Page